AN EASY GUIDE TO ARTIFICIAL LIGHT-GARDENING
FOR PLEASURE AND PROFIT

AN EASY GUIDE TO
Artificial Light-Gardening
FOR PLEASURE AND PROFIT

by

VERNON JOHNSTON and WINIFRED CARRIERE

drawings by **BOB DARA**

photographs by **STUART FOX**
(except Plates VI, VII, VIII)

GRAMERCY PUBLISHING COMPANY
NEW YORK

To Mickey

ACKNOWLEDGMENTS

We gratefully acknowledge the assistance of our many light-gardening friends in preparing this book. We especially wish to thank the following for their extensive cooperation: Cristos C. Mpelkas, Sylvania Electric Products, for checking technicalities; Peter Brown, Sylvania Electric Products, for assistance with photographs; Mrs. Muriel Orans, American Geranium Society; Dr. J. George Milstein, New York Bromeliad Society; Mr. & Mrs. Thomas Powell, Lager & Hurrell, for information on orchids; Mr. R. B. Farnham, the Horticultural Society of New York; Miss Anne Marie Birdsey, Brooklyn Botanic Garden; Mrs. Hope Ireland, the African Violet Society; Mr. Mal Kuhn, formerly of W. Atlee Burpee Company; the Brooklyn Botanical Society; Mr. E. R. Hall, Knickerbocker Begonia Society; and most especially, Nedda Anders of Hearthside Press, who became a light-gardener as we worked together.

Winifred Carrière
Vernon Johnston

New York, February 1964

TABLE OF CONTENTS

PART I

The Pleasure of Light-Gardening

If you care about plants, gardening under lights should appeal to you. Whatever your interest in gardening—if you are impatient with seasons, or are an apartment horticulturist, or want the very biggest and best specimen in the flower show, even if you hope to make pin money from a pleasurable pastime—we believe that light-gardening is the answer. It offers a reasonable certainty of success even to those who have never grown so much as a pot of greenery.

As so many of us have learned, window-sill gardening has its limitations, particularly for apartment dwellers. Few apartments offer all four exposures, and the available window sills may not be facing in a plant-oriented direction. Surrounding buildings may cut off the light until too late in the day to benefit plants, even in favored exposures. And even ideally located window sills are at right angles to straight upright glass panes, from which the light bounces off at an angle. (Greenhouses have slanted panes because more light can go *through* them.) *We* can see an abundance of light through our window glass, but the plants cannot receive the energy they need through unslanted, upright panes. Too, modern heating systems and city smog coat the glass when windows are closed in the winter. This coating prevents beneficial light rays from reaching plants, especially through the oil and dust that cover the leaves and deprive them of humidity from the atmosphere. Light-gardening is a solution to the problems of window-sill gardeners.

Since plants cannot live by light alone, we have included information about soils and soil substitutes, watering (hand and automatic), feeding both young and mature plants even when you are on vacation, and making a light-garden attractive enough to be a decorative asset in your home. We have suggested plants to grow under lights according to your individual purposes, and taken a look into the future at experiments you may enjoy making.

We—both authors—are impatient gardeners. We garden under lights as a part-time hobby, motivated by the fact that winter is far too long, as it always is for enthusiastic gardeners. In this book, we pass along to you what we have learned from our own experiences, from other light-gardeners, and from the questions posed by interested members of the audiences who attend our lectures. Their questions have focussed our attention on the obvious and less-obvious problems that plague beginners. We have tried to give some of the answers, but we do not claim omniscience. Therefore we urge you to experiment on your own, and to keep up with new information in this young field through books and magazines.

In the Johnston home in central New Jersey, plants have been grown under lights for the past eight or nine winters, to be transplanted out of doors, often in full bloom, as soon as the ground is ready. The Johnston light-garden is in the lower level of a one-family home, close to the outdoor garden area which has the unusual combination of fertile soil and seaside atmosphere. When the gardens need attention, there is always someone at home to do whatever is needed.

In the Carrière apartment in midtown Manhattan, there is quite a different situation. This is a typical New York apartment, far from ideal for plant growth, in which absentee gardening is the rule rather than the exception. But light-gardening is a year-round source of gardening enjoyment.

Plants here are further menaced by Siamese cats, who prefer a tender shoot to cat food. The outdoor Carrière garden in southwestern Connecticut, tended only on weekends, is the ultimate home and also the source of supply for many of the plants grown in the New York light-garden. Located sixty miles out of the City, its rocky soil and heavily shaded area present problems of their own. And in the office of Johnston & Carrière, Inc., also in midtown Manhattan, plants are grown under lights during the week, and left to their own devices for weekends.

These are our light-gardens. We love them, and find that they satisfy our hunger for longer-lasting gardening pleasures. Perhaps you would like a light-garden for another purpose: for growing orchids or gesneriads, for raising fragrant herbs in a dark kitchen, or for cultivating decorative plants to adorn the living room. Whatever the reason, we hope that this book will help you get started.

1

Light and Darkness in Plant Growth

Every gardener knows that not all plants react similarly to a given condition. Jungle plants, for instance, grow out of soil that never has a chance to dry out, under such tall trees that the light that reaches them is always filtered through dense overhead foliage. At the other extreme are plants that live in high altitudes or in brilliant desert lights, with no trees to shelter them and so little water in the sand they grow in that they almost have to belong to the cactus family to survive at all.

The vast majority of plants grown out of doors in home gardens, however, fall into the middle category. They grow their roots in what gardeners know to be nourishing soil, with the recommended amount of moisture both around their roots and in the atmosphere, and with some relief from either too much or too little sunshine.

SIMULATING NATURE—THE THEORY BEHIND LIGHT-GARDENING

In light-gardening, we are interested primarily in how man can make plants react indoors as though they were growing under nature's own outdoor conditions. Several years ago, it was observed that the leaves on trees growing near lighted street lamps came out earlier than the leaves on unlighted

14

trees. This discovery focussed attention on the overwhelming importance of light to plant growth. In subsequent research, scientists at the U. S. Department of Agriculture in Beltsville, Maryland, were able to isolate the pigment that governs the reaction of plant life to light. They named this pigment phytochrome. Investigation of its effect on plants is still going on, but knowledge of its existence opened the way to an entire new concept of horticulture.

WHY PLANTS GROW

Basically, the cycle of plant life works like this: the rays of the sun, striking the chlorophyll-filled green leaves of a plant, wake up the plant. Thus activated, the chlorophyll begins converting into energy-producing starch (carbohydrates) the sugars, fats, proteins, and minerals that the roots find when they burrow into fertile ground—and the pumping chain reaction of plant growth is set in motion. Without chlorophyll, nothing productive happens, because only the chlorophyll in plants converts sugar into starch.

WHY PLANTS NEED DARKNESS

While the light is creating all this activity, the plant is so busy responding that it finds relatively little time to make use of the foods it is manufacturing for growth. Only when the light is gone and night falls, natural or induced, does the plant have an opportunity for cell growth. If light kept the plant busy around the clock, the plant would probably die of overexertion. In the world that we know, there are day and night in each twenty-four hours, and there are four seasons each year. Plants grow for us under these conditions.

House plants and annuals seem to need darkness during their blooming periods. Very recent reports from the University of Connecticut indicate that woody shrubs and trees can stand *some* light round the clock, but the high intensities of noonday light cannot be continuous. So the plant hobbyist must simulate the lighting conditions of night and day and sometimes of the four seasons. He is now doing this by means of electricity, most conveniently provided in light-gardens.

THE COLORS OF LIGHT THAT AFFECT PLANT GROWTH

Knowing how plants react to light and dark and to seasons, scientists decided to see how plants react to specific colors of light. Each color of light has its own wave length, and plants were discovered to be most responsive to red and blue wave lengths. How much the other color bands support, reinforce, or contribute to plant growth has not yet been established. We know, however, that *red light* stimulates bloom and vegetative growth, causing plants to become tall; and that *blue light* both regulates the respiratory system and makes the plants grow bushier.

This conclusion upset a useful light-measurement system. Scientists had been accustomed to measuring light in terms of foot candles, an arbitrary term that serves much the same function as horsepower. Foot candles is a measurement of visual light in its entire spectrum. It is not a divisible measurement that can be used to determine any one color of light in the spectrum. Since we are concerned here with only the red and blue wave lengths, we have avoided using foot candles as a point of reference in this book.

TECHNICAL TERMS

We have tried to avoid laboratory terminology as much as possible, but a few technical words are necessary. Scientists always develop a specialized vocabulary as a kind of shorthand, and those who have studied light and its effect on plants are no exception. From the Greek word "photon", meaning light, has come *photosynthesis*, which may be defined as food conversion by light; *phototropism*, attraction to light; and *photoperiodism,* timing by light. *(Photography* means writing with light.)

Phototropism denotes the involuntary movement of plants in turning their leaf and flower faces always toward the light. *Photoperiodism* describes the requirement of plants for alternate periods of light and dark, which directly affects flowering and fruiting.

PHOTOPERIODISM APPLIED

Photoperiodism needs more than mere definition, for if you know the photoperiod of a given plant, you can simulate it with artificial light to encourage or retard the flowering and fruiting of that plant. Photoperiodism is correlated with length of season, characterized by short-day or long-day growth habits. In general, tropical plants are short-day plants; subarctic and high-altitude plants are long-day plants; and temperate-zone plants are usually intermediate.

Short-day and long-day are actually misnomers, since it is the length of the night or period of darkness, rather than the length of the light period, that governs plant growth. But the terms have developed in describing the photoperiod of plants that normally flower in fall and winter when days are short, as opposed to those that bloom during the long hours of daylight in the summer. In light-garden application, a short day is only eight to ten hours of light; a long day, fourteen to sixteen hours.

In a curious development of creating dark and light periods for plants, it was established that many plants are so sensitive to light that if the dark period is interrupted in the middle by only a few minutes of light, these plants react as if a new day had started. Now it seems likely that only a few *seconds* of light interjected around midnight may be enough to cause this reaction. Studies of the subject are continuing, but it is known that if the dark period of a short-day plant is broken with light around midnight, the plant may refuse to flower.

SHORT-DAY PLANTS

Among the short-day plants are:

Asters	Kalanchoe
Bromeliads	Marigolds
Christmas Cactus	Poinsettia
Chrysanthemums	Primula
Cosmos	Salvia
Dracaena	Sansevieria
Freesia	Zinnia

LONG-DAY PLANTS

Long-day plants, exposed to light in the middle of the night, may bloom sooner than normal. Long-day plants appear to need a longer light interruption, and more specific conclusions have been reached about the short-day plants. Again, the matter is under continuous study by plant scientists. Some long-day plants such as bachelors-button, coreopsis, forget-me-not, phlox, rudbeckia, salpiglossis, scabiosa, snapdragon, verbena, and others listed in Part II will grow better at the *seedling* stage if put on a short-day schedule. They will then produce shorter stems.

Among the long-day plants are:

Azalea	Fuchsia
Begonia (Tuberous)	Heather
Cacti	Helianthus (sunflower)
China aster	Hydrangea
Cineraria	Lilies
Crotons	Nasturtium
Dahlia	Petunia
Delphinium	Roses
Dianthus	Saintpaulias
Digitalis (foxglove)	Stock
Gardenia	Violets

vegetables, such as beans and spinach

Woody plants are similarly affected by photoperiodism. In

natural outdoor conditions, as autumn progresses and nights lengthen, woody plants cease to elongate their stems, and concentrate on hardening off in self-protection against winter cold. It is possible to persuade many woody plants to continue to grow during the naturally short days of winter by giving them long-day lighting. U.S.D.A. researchers working on this aspect of plant growth at Beltsville have found it useful to add incandescent lamps to their fluorescent lights for woody plants.

THE INTERMEDIATES

The majority of plants have no rigid photoperiod requirements. They do well under a wide range of day lengths, and respond to an even distribution of twelve hours of light and twelve of darkness. Sometimes classed as day-neutrals, this group can be grown happily in your light-garden together with the more exacting long- and short-day plants. They may perhaps be speeded or slowed somewhat by having more or less light than they actually need, but their bloom will not be prevented.

COMBINING DAY LENGTHS IN YOUR LIGHT-GARDEN

Plants are more adaptable than one would expect. You can grow long- and short-day plants together, just as nature does outdoors. The vegetative growth of short-day plants, mums and poinsettias, for example, is beautiful amid flowering long-day plants. But when the time comes that you want any plant to flower, you have to give it the specific photoperiod that it requires.

In a light-garden, you control day length simply by turning off the lights after the desired number of hours. When you grow both long-day and short-day plants in the same light-garden, the short-day plants are either removed after their prescribed number of hours and put in a dark place, or covered with an opaque black shading cloth.

Figure 1   Removing a tray of short-day plants from the light-garden after their prescribed number of hours. (A rolling table or teacart makes the job easier.) Alternative is to cover them with a shading cloth.

In Part II we discuss some interesting controls of blooming time in such plants as poinsettia and chrysanthemum, but the principle of speeding or delaying bloom in light-gardening can be widely applied to a variety of plants providing you understand their natural photoperiodism.

2

Lamps and Equipment for Man-made Sunshine

To apply the theories of the effect of light on plants, scientists experimented with various types of electric light. The U. S. Department of Agriculture at its Beltsville, Maryland station pioneered in this field, setting up a variety of conditions for testing plant growth under incandescent and fluorescent lights. Keeping pace with the Beltsville discoveries, and simultaneously running their own laboratory tests, the large manufacturers of lighting equipment developed lamps designed specifically for indoor gardening. As a result, indoor gardening for both the amateur and the commercial grower has been revolutionized.

FLUORESCENT LAMPS

Basically, a light-garden is a place for growing plants under artificial light. Fluorescent tubes are the major source of this light, but incandescent (filament) bulbs are still widely used as auxiliaries.

Fluorescent tubes are available in standard lengths: 18-, 24-, 36-, 48-, 72-, and 96-inch lengths that provide from 15 to 215 watts. Long straight tubes, twisted tubes, and circular tubes that are useful where space is limited, as in a corner, are available. For light-gardening, they all need a reflector to focus the light onto the plants beneath them. Some tubes have a built-in reflector coated with titanium oxide. They are primarily useful if plants are located, for decorative reasons, some distance from the light source. By narrowing the area where the light falls, the built-in reflector increases the intensity of light to make up for the greater distance it must travel to reach the plants. For most purposes, the plant-oriented choice of standard fluorescent lamps by color, installed in a fixture or pan with reflecting shades, is adequate.

The choice of colors useful in plant growth is a wide one, including natural white, warm white, deluxe warm white, soft white, cool white, deluxe cool white, and daylight. The cool shades such as daylight are more blue than the warm shades such as warm white, which contain more red. Therefore a combination of one warm white and one daylight tube is generally recommended for plant growth. But if your light-garden is set into a natural light situation like a north window, where the lamps are used merely to extend the length of day, you might prefer only warm tones of white tubes.

In setting up lamps to supplement natural light, it must be recognized that not much more than 40 percent of the light rays that reach a window go through the glass to reach the plants. And on overcast days or short-light days from late fall until late spring, nature does not provide the light that most plants need for flowering.

PLANT-GROWTH FLUORESCENTS

Special fluorescents designed for plant growth are now available. They combine the red and the blue in proper balance within the same tube. Where two standards in different colors usually are required to provide this balance of red and blue, a single plant-growth fluorescent does the job. These special lamps are more effective than the combined standard lamps. Although these fluorescents cost approximately twice as much as standard tubes, they seem to be well worth it, because they concentrate on producing the plant-stimulating light, wasting none of their energy on colors to which plants appear to be unresponsive. Plant-growth lamps are available in 24-, 48-, or 96-inch lengths, rated at 20, 40, and 73 watts, respectively. Sylvania Electric Products was first to develop these lamps, and now markets them under the trade name of Gro-Lux.

We have found these plant-growth fluorescents superior to standard ones for starting seeds, rooting cuttings, and in general for getting things growing. But there is still a question in our minds as to whether all plants *continue* to grow to their fullest bloom and production under plant-growth lights. We have never had a plant stop growing under a proper combination of standard fluorescents, although it may have started growing more slowly than it would under plant-growth light. But under the plant-growth lights, we have found that some plants appear to go into a state of trance, holding the pose as it were. This is particularly true of the light-loving plants listed in Part II.

Standard fluorescents do not appreciably affect the visible color of flowers or foliage; but plant-growth lamps cast a lavender tone that gives the plants a not unpleasant although rather unnatural color. The energy that plant-growth lamps produce for growing purposes cannot be measured accurately with a light-meter in terms of foot candles, as we explained in chapter 1, and only the plants themselves can tell you clearly whether they are receiving the light they need.

Plant-growth fluorescents fit into the same fixtures as standard fluorescents, and may be interchanged. In all cases, they need a reflecting surface above them. The light produced from the three or four inches at each end of *any* fluorescent tube is less efficient for plant growth than that from the center of the tube, so a longer span of efficient light is provided without interruption by the longer tubes.

HOW MUCH LIGHT FROM THE LAMPS

A good rule of thumb is to provide 10 to 20 watts of plant-

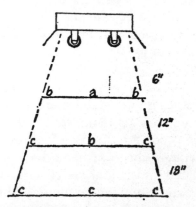

Figure 2   The highest light intensity is in the six inches directly below each lamp where the light rays converge. This is zone *a* on the sketch. Intensity diminishes as the distance from the lamps increases, both in the center of the shelf and at the edges, zone *b*. But at eighteen inches directly below each lamp, intensity is almost the same as at the ends of the tubes, zone *c*. Light-loving plants do best in zone *a;* those that prefer partial shade outdoors, in zone *b;* and shade-preferring plants belong in zone *c*.

growth fluorescent light, or 20 to 40 watts of combined standard fluorescents, for each square foot of light-garden area. Of course, plants differ in their need for light, but their preferences are accommodated by arranging their distance from the light source. A square foot of light will accommodate approximately forty-eight seedlings from sprouting to the time they are ready to transplant; or four mature plants six inches in diameter.

INCANDESCENT (FILAMENT) LAMPS

Although many light-gardeners still use two or three low-wattage incandescent bulbs to supplement their standard fluorescent tubes, we consider them old-fashioned and unnecessary. Incandescents are spotty in distributing light, and give off too much heat for most plants. Because high temperature and insufficient humidity will kill more plants than all the insects in the insect kingdom, we decided to try growing our plants without the lamps that raise temperature and dry out the air. In nine years of light-gardening, we have had spectacular success without using any incandescents, simply because fluorescent lamps do the job more than adequately for the average light-gardener.

Originally, incandescent lamps were added to fluorescents to provide additional infra-red light, which some plants need for blooming. Large-scale growers who need to accelerate the blooming time of their plants to meet commercial seasons; hybridizers who wish to speed up their seed settings; and specialists who grow woody plants may find incandescents helpful.

If incandescent light seems to be needed, we suggest investigating the recent application to light-gardening of an old lighting principle. It was brought to our attention by E. R. Hall of Brooklyn, N. Y., a lighting engineer who specializes in theater lighting and is an enthusiastic light-gardener. Because he is particularly interested in developing new plants through hybridization, he felt a need for additional infra-red light that would not burn his tender seedlings. Familiarity with the "long-life" bulbs used in inaccessible theater ceilings led him to successful experimentation in his light-garden.

"Long-life" incandescent bulbs suitable for light-garden use are 15-watt bulbs that can use 135 volts of electricity. Screwed into the normal 120-volt light socket, they burn cooler than ordinary incandescents, give off less visible light than an ordinary 15-watt bulb, and produce more infra-red rays. They cost about four times as much as an ordinary bulb of the same wattage, but since they almost never have to be replaced, their cost is a minor consideration. And although

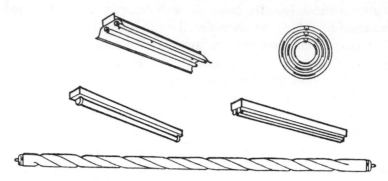

Figure 3   Top left: a 2-channel industrial fixture with built-on reflector; Top right: a triple circular fixture; Center: a 1-channel and a
2-channel fixture; Bottom: a Power-Twist tube.

they do use more current than an ordinary bulb, the cost of
operating the few high-voltage bulbs you would need in a
light-garden is also insignificant. Literally, they burn for
years without replacement.

FLUORESCENT-LAMP FIXTURES

Fluorescent tubes are housed in neat little white metal boxes
or pans that come complete with connectors into which the
tubes fit easily. The housing above the tubes has predrilled
holes so that it can be screwed into any ceiling, shelf bottom,
or whatever.

Each set of one tube and its connectors is called a channel,
and fluorescent fixtures are available in 1-, 2-, 3-, or 4-channel
widths. The length of the tube governs the wattage, and accordingly, the higher the wattage, the longer the tube. A 20-
watt tube is 24 inches long.

REFLECTORS

In addition to the tubes and the fixture or pan that holds
them, a reflecting surface of some kind is essential, as we have

mentioned earlier. Its purpose is to diffuse the light downward over the plants. Any "roof" or ceiling into which the light is screwed becomes a good reflecting surface if painted with flat-white paint. Contrary to expectations, a flat-white surface diffuses more light than does a gloss white or polished aluminum.

Some fluorescent fixtures made for industrial use have built-on reflectors over them. These reflectors are slanted so that they confine the light to the area directly under them, diffusing it somewhat as it spreads outward from the center. If you use such a fixture, paint the inside of the reflector with flat white.

You can contrive your own reflector from plywood, masonite, or similar materials, as detailed in chapter 3. Just be sure to paint the part above the tubes with flat white, and to keep the reflector no more than a foot above the lamps, or the light that travels upward will be lost.

PORTABLE LIGHT-GARDENS

Now that light-gardening is becoming an important hobby, lamp manufacturers are making portable setups in various price ranges. There is not yet a very large variety of shapes and sizes in these ready-made units, but they can be found in some garden shops and department stores, and in most garden mail-order catalogs. Major lamp manufacturers can advise you of what is currently on the market, and where to find it.

Among the ready-made light-gardens are some that are adjustable, so that the light fixture can be raised or lowered to the desired distance above the plants—a very desirable feature in any light-garden. Others are at a fixed height. Some are made with planters in the bottom; some without. Some have miniature greenhouses over them. Some are purely utilitarian, others are more decorative. Styles include wheeled carts, terrariums, floor-standing and table models, and hanging planters.

If you decide to buy a ready-made light-garden, be sure to choose a fixture that does not have a push-button starter to be held down until the light goes on. This type of fixture, reminiscent of the earliest of the fluorescent desk lamps, cannot be adapted to automatic timers and waterers; and sooner or later, you are likely to want automation. Of course, if you are interested only in having a few green plants growing in a pin-up lamp, automation is not important.

LONGEVITY OF LAMPS

Normally, lamps will last from one to two years. They have a use expectancy of from ten to twenty thousand hours, if you turn them on and off only once or twice a day. But *maximum* efficiency, which is what your plants need, is only about half of the visible-light efficiency of the tube. When the tubes are not producing enough light for the plants, the plants will stop growing and blooming normally and healthfully.

If you have a light-meter, take a reading of the light from each tube when you install it. Record the reading, and in about six months, take another for comparison. When the reading goes down to half of the original light output, it's time to replace the tube, even though it may still look perfectly efficient to your eyes. Without a light-meter, the plants themselves will tell you when it's time for a change. But of course, there could be some other reason why they look unhappy, and if three days under a new tube produces no improvement, look for the real cause of the difficulty.

HOW TO INCREASE LIGHT INTENSITY

No matter what plants you are growing, you probably will find it desirable at times to change the amount of light they are receiving. Sometimes just a longer day, up to sixteen hours, may do the trick. Young, immature plants, even short-day ones, need more light than mature plants. And seedlings should be closer to the source of light than developed plants.

When you are convinced that all or some of your plants need more light, you can increase the intensity in these ways: Raise the plants closer to the lamps (fluorescents are cool and won't burn the plants); lower the lights if you have an adjustable arrangement; move the plants so that they are just below the center of the tubes, where the light is more intense than at the ends; add more lamps; or replace tubes that have been in use for six or seven thousand hours.

CARE AND MAINTENANCE

Manufacturers recommend that you leave the tubes alone, once you've installed them. But if dust has obviously accumulated on them, wipe it off. If the reflector looks grey, repaint it. There is nothing else that is likely to give you extra housekeeping chores except the plants themselves. At the end of this chapter, some typical maintenance questions are answered.

THE COST

Man-made sunshine, obviously, is as easy to provide as the electric light by which you read. The cost of the tubes is low in terms of initial investment, and two 40-watt lamps for a basic setup will total only a few dollars. The pans or fixtures are more expensive, but their cost is hardly prohibitive. All the equipment is readily available.

Because cost of electric current varies with the amount you use, as well as from region to region, it is impossible for us to state exactly how much your hobby will add to your light bill. But your local power company can give you specific information, and at the same time make certain that you are not overloading your electric circuits. We would guess that the annual cost of lighting your indoor garden will come to "the low two figures", as banks put it—certainly a trifling amount for the pleasure you will derive from it.

ANSWERS TO QUESTIONS ABOUT FLUORESCENT LAMPS

Q. *If I accidentally break a tube, will dangerous gas escape?*

A. No. Modern fluorescents present no danger when broken except possible glass cuts. Pick up the pieces with a wet paper towel to protect your fingers.

Q. *Does the tube need replacing when it has black rings around the ends?*

A. Not necessarily, but if you know the tube is more than a year old and has been constantly in use, black rings may indicate the need for a change. Check its light production as we have suggested, and compare it with the production you recorded when it was first installed.

Q. *What do you do when a tube flickers?*

A. First, replace the starter. It may have burned out. If the tube is a relatively new one, it should no longer flicker unless the ballasts need replacing—an electrician's job. If it's an old tube, replace it; if this doesn't help, call an electrician.

Q. *How do you figure the total current used by the light-garden?*

A. Add the wattages printed on the ends of each tube. To the result, add an extra one-fourth of the total.

Q. *Can I use ordinary fluorescent tubes in a greenhouse kept at 40° F.?*

A. You can, but they will be less efficient. There are special lamps designed for low temperatures under 50° F. If you use ordinary lamps, build a heat-holding envelope around it.

Q. Can I save on my light bill by turning the lights on and off frequently?

A. No. It takes much more electric current to start the lamp than to burn it. The longer the period during which the lamp is kept lighted, the more economical is its use.

Q. How can I be sure I'm not overloading my electric circuits?

A. Only an electrician can tell you. But if your fuses consistently blow out, you can be sure that you have an overload.

3

Constructing a Light-Garden

Artificial lights may be used alone or in combination with natural daylight. But when used alone, your plants have better form because the light comes from above them. It is the leaf tips of plants that are most responsive to light, and plants set into a window need an occasional quarter turn to keep them from growing lopsided. Aside from this consideration, placement of your light-garden can be almost anywhere, if you observe the basic conditions that make plants grow well.

THE BASIC CONDITIONS

1. Choose an airy but not drafty location. Drafty doors, windows, any passageways—any architectural arrangement that can create a sudden temperature change—should be avoided. If you must place your garden where drafts can reach it, set up a screen as protection. Insulate drafty windows in winter by using plastic strips that fit between glass and frame; they are just lifted out in the spring when the windows are opened.

Dead-air corners are also menacing, and can be eliminated simply by plugging in a small slow-moving electric fan, set to blow against a wall in the light-garden to create air circulation. A simple way to discover drafts and dead-air corners is to blow tobacco smoke or incense into the air of the room, and watch its motion and drift against the light. You will see that it swirls or hovers in definite patterns, according to the way the air circulates in the room. If it hovers, almost motionless, in one place, that place is a dead-air corner. If it rushes invariably in one direction—toward a door or window —a draft is present. Provide an exhaust fan or air-conditioning where it will pull the air away from a dead-air corner. In the Carrière apartment, where the living room air-conditioner is twenty feet away from the light-garden, we find the plants healthier when the air-conditioner is in use. It is set on exhaust in winter, and on exhaust-cool in summer whenever the air seems stuffy (here we apply only the nose test).

2. *Avoid excessive heat.* The plant setup should be placed as far away as possible from the heating outlets. The closer it gets to heat, the more humidity you will have to supply, which means that maintenance can become a real chore. However, a radiator does make an attractive spot for the light-garden and one such garden is described later in this chapter.

Often the ideal combination of draft-free and correct-heat environment does not exist, but it *is* possible to overcome most of the dangers from the heating system, and to provide enough relative humidity to satisfy both plants and people. We detail additional methods in the chapter on care and feeding of light-garden plants.

3. *Conceal the light tubes.* If the light-garden is part of your living area, you will want to place the tubes so that they don't shine in your eyes. This can be accomplished in several different ways. The light tubes can be set up below eye level (as in a fireplace installation); they can be shielded behind architectural beams of the kind one often finds in early-American houses or lovely old Tudors; or they can be used unobtrusively in furniture. The installation can also be concealed with a cornice or valance.

4. Consider the temperature. Most plants have a wide tolerance in their native habitat; for example, African violets will grow at a temperature as low as 40° F. and as high as 80° F. Gloxinias seem to thrive best at 62° F., but what human being likes a daytime temperature as low as that? It is fortunate that plants are adaptable. You can grow a wide range of plants indoors with a day temperature up to about 75° F., and a night temperature lower by about 10 or 15 degrees. The list in Part II will help you choose.

INSTALLING THE EQUIPMENT

The fixtures for fluorescent tubes are about an inch and a half longer than the tubes they hold. You need a little space in which to work as you install the fixtures, so it's best to have an extra two or three inches of *interior* space at both ends of the tubes when you attach them inside an area that has side walls, such as a bookcase.

For example, if you have a bookcase that is 54 inches wide, count yourself lucky. Your 48-inch tubes in their 51-inch fixture will fit nicely. The fixtures and tubes are the only really essential elements of your light-garden that are inflexible. You have to take what you can buy, but you can adjust the distance between shelves to suit your needs. Lamp stores have attractive pulley arrangements that make it possible for you to hang your lamps above the top of the garden on chains, raising or lowering them. And adjustable shelves provide added flexibility in accommodating their positions to the height of growing plants.

If one or more of your light-garden shelves is immovable, be sure to allow enough space to accommodate the plants you want to grow under it. You need from six to ten inches from the top leaves of the plant to the bottom of the fluorescent tubes, and a practicable rule of thumb is to allow at least two feet between shelves. Just don't forget to consider the height of your largest container, the height of your tallest

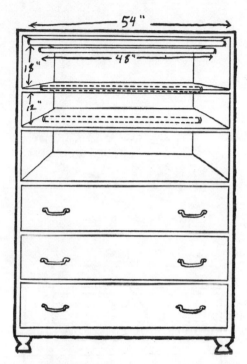

Figure 4   In a bookcase 54 inches wide, 48-inch tubes in a 51-inch fixture will fit nicely. Allow an extra two or three inches of interior space at both ends of the tubes for easy installation.

plant, and the four inches of space taken up by fixtures and tubes, as well as the distance from top leaves to tubes.

A BASIC LIGHT-GARDEN SETUP

For a beginning, you can use a sturdy table or bench. Two 40-watt fluorescent lamps, one warm white and one cool white in a double channel four feet long, can then be suspended on a pulley chain over the table. Later, you may want

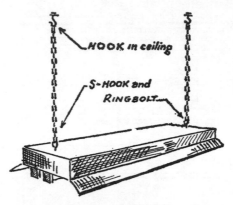

CHAIN METHOD

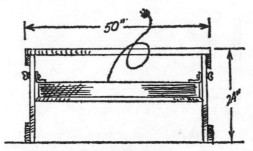

FRONT VIEW OF
LIGHT RIG WITH LEGS

SIDE VIEW

Figure 5   Two methods for install-
ing adjustable lamps. Top: Chains
hooked to ceiling can be shortened
by moving S-hook up to higher
links. Center and bottom: Self-
supporting rig. To make: Use two
boards 2″ x ¾″ fastened to bases
that can be screwed to top of table
holding plants. Space them to
allow ¼″ slot between boards (see
side view of support); connect with
board across top. Screw angle iron
to top of lamp fixture on each end.
Screw 2-inch stove bolts into free ends of angle irons, insert bolts into
slots. Tighten with wing nuts. Fluorescent light can be lowered or
raised to connecting board across top by loosening screws.

to change to plant-growth tubes. You must provide a reflector, either of the industrial type or a homemade one.

MINIMUM EQUIPMENT

For convenient light-gardening, you'll need:

Rustproof trays about two inches deep to hold plant containers. Pour in pebbles one inch deep. Keep pebbles almost covered with water to provide necessary humidity. A humidity gauge is not absolutely essential, but helpful.

Stands, boxes, flats, containers. We especially like containers that nest for easy storage when not in use.

Peat-pot strips.

Gravel or broken clay pots for drainage in the bottoms of containers.

Potting mixture, vermiculite, perlite (see the all-purpose soil recipe in chapter 5).

A small plastic fork for aerating top soil.

A pencil or stick for dibbling in plants.

A large watering can and a hand mist sprayer.

A small trowel, sugar scoop or large spoon for transplanting; measuring cups and spoons for fertilizer; polyethylene bags for covering newly planted seeds.

Brushes, sponges, and a litter basket for clean-up work.

BUILDING A LIGHT GARDEN WHERE IT FITS

In many ways, it is easier to build a fluorescent light-garden from scratch, getting the fluorescent equipment first and then constructing around it. When you build one, remember to buy the longest tubes you can fit into the space you plan, because the most light energy comes from the center of the tube. In a long tube, there is more center, and therefore more effective lighting.

If you live in an apartment, it is almost inevitable that your light-garden will be placed in a conspicuous part of the room it occupies. And if you are the typical home owner, it is almost as inevitable that the hobby will start in the basement or garage, but soon encroach on the living quarters upstairs, for you will want a place to exhibit those wonderful plants you are growing, and to keep them healthy while they are showing. This means you'll just have to have more lights upstairs!

HOW HIGH CAN THE LIGHTS BE PLACED?

In Part II, we answer this question in relation to specific plants, but let us suppose that you want to install a small circular fluorescent-light fixture in a corner of the room, where it can be concealed by a beam about seven or eight feet high. Under this light you have a perfect spot for growing a light-loving plant in a hanging basket. The top of the plant should be about eight to twelve inches below the light.

If you specialize in miniatures, you can space your light-garden shelves approximately eighteen inches apart. This will place the tubes eight or ten inches above the tops of the plants. But if you go in for tall chrysanthemums, you'll need an extra foot or two between the shelves. And if you plan a miscellaneous garden with plants of varying heights, gear the shelf distance to the needs of your tallest plants, and elevate the lower ones to the height *they* need. The absolute minimum working distance between shelves is one foot (and this only for seedlings and rooting cuttings).

IMAGINATIVE PLACEMENTS

Possibilities are endless for adapting old furniture. If you find you are squeezed for height above your plants, you can save a couple of inches by having the fluorescent mechanism hooked up by remote ballast. Any electrician can do it for you; don't attempt to do it yourself.

A *Whatnot:* A corner whatnot could be delightful for mini-

Figure 6 You can adapt a bookcase, record cabinet, or discarded
vanity table to light-garden use. A bookcase with adjustable shelves
is ideal.

ature plants no more than six inches tall at maturity. Paint
the undersides of the shelves with flat white to make them
reflectors. Secure circular fluorescent tubes under the shelves.
For greater light intensity, double or triple circles, one inside the other, will do the job. Since a whatnot is open on
both of its triangular sides, it provides plenty of air circulation, but you'll need to check its location to be sure it is not
a dead-air corner.

A *Bookcase:* You can adapt a bookcase or record cabinet
in the same way, using single or multi-channel fixtures
fastened under the shelves. You may have to take out one
shelf, if they are only normally far apart (ten inches), in order
to accommodate your taller plants. A bookcase with adjustable shelves is ideal. All you have to do with a solid-backed
bookcase is to paint the inside to reflect light, and open the
back or sides sufficiently to allow for air circulation. You can
saw out parts of the back, or drill holes at both sides and

rear. Filigree panelboard or cross bars can be used to replace the entire back, if removing the original back endangers the sturdiness of the structure. Place the bookcase light-garden about two inches away from the wall, so that air can circulate freely behind it.

A Window Alcove: We recently helped to install a supplementary light-garden in the home of a friend. In a charming, quite cool room, a recessed casement window became a focal point. We covered a shelf with "walnut" formica, added a five-inch apron in front, and painted the underside

Figure 7   A built-in bookcase is another good place for a light-garden. Just be sure to provide air circulation by drilling holes in sides.

of the shelf with flat white paint. Then we installed a two-channel fluorescent fixture under the shelf, holding 40-watt tubes. The installation is hidden by the apron. On the floor below the shelf, our friend now displays a magnificent collection of gloxinias. On the shelf top are climbing and trailing philodendron plants, getting the little light they need from the north window, which is shaded by a large rhododendron growing outside.

A *Radiator Top:* A light-garden on top of a radiator has the dual purpose of concealing an eyesore and creating an area of beauty, but you have to overcome the danger from the heating system. A sheet of asbestos between the radiator and the light-garden shelf helps keep the plants from drying. The shelf is a lead or zinc tray about two inches deep, holding a one-inch layer of pebbles that are constantly kept watered to provide humidity.

A *Fireplace:* An unused fireplace is an excellent spot for a light-garden, either permanently or just for the summer.

Figure 8 An unused fireplace is ideal for a light-garden. You may need to install a small, slow-rotating fan to keep air circulating properly.

A frame of aluminum tubing can be constructed to fit the shelves into the tapering depth of the space; or you can set a portable light-garden into it. Either will be easy to remove when you want to use the fireplace again on a chilly night. But be certain to eliminate any draft created by the chimney. A sheet of plywood fitted into the chimney opening will seal it. Then check for air circulation, and if necessary, install a 4-inch slow-moving fan.

A Kitchen Cabinet: It's a simple matter to install two 40-watt lights under a top bank of kitchen cabinets. Some cabinets have a slight overhang that will conceal the installation, but if yours don't have it, add a strip of decorative molding. A row of potted herbs set on the base cabinets below the lights will delight the gourmet gardener. But don't be tempted to grow flowering plants near a gas oven. Even the smallest amount of gas fumes is poisonous to geraniums and many other flowering plants.

In the Greenhouse: It is possible to just about double working space in a greenhouse if you attach fluorescents under the benches. Here you can grow the plants suited to the available temperature and humidity. There is no limit to the possibilities for creating light-gardens to satisfy your longing for off-season plants if you just remember the essentials of good growing conditions—such as temperature, air circulation, and humidity. In a cool greenhouse (below 50° F.), special fluorescent tubes are useful.

THE JOHNSTON LIGHT-GARDEN

Perhaps the most explicit descriptions can be based on our own two light-gardens. The first was built in the lower level of the Johnston home in Ocean County, New Jersey. It is a delightful indoor terrace. In fact, this garden under lights has become a showplace and gathering spot for the Johnstons' friends and *their* friends; even strangers come and ask to see the Johnston "winter garden." As often happens, accident played a part in its construction. The local lumberyard hap-

pened to be renovating its showroom, and sold us their fluorescent fixtures and tubes (which burned out shortly) for next
to nothing. The fixtures are the most expensive item in the
whole cost of a light-garden, and these were four-footers in
perfect working order. We dug out of the attic an old pede-
stal-type vanity table with two drawers, and a pair of record
cabinets with vertical dividers. They were all the same
height, and did beautifully as supports for a couple of solid
wooden batten boards that were no longer needed as hurri-
cane protection over windows.

We cut the vanity apart, took out the drawers, and used
the pedestal bases to support one of the batten boards. Under
the other board, we put the two record cabinets, one under
each end. This gave us two side-by-side light-gardens, four
feet wide, two-and-a-half feet deep, and just the right height
to make a working surface at counter level. At either end of
both setups, we erected three two-by-twos, notched an inch
deep at three-inch intervals on the insides. The notches provide support for shelves of three-quarter-inch plywood, two
feet wide.

The basement ceiling beams were high enough to permit
setting up three growing levels. There's a fixed set of tubes
attached directly to the beams, and room for two movable
shelves between the fixed tubes and the fixed shelf atop the
pedestals. Each movable shelf has fluorescents fastened
under it, to light the plants below. If we should need them
for very small plants, we can always add shelves between, or
under the fixed top on the pedestals. As it is, we have eighty
square feet of light-garden that can be adjusted to the needs
of our plants—plus plenty of working space at all levels, and
storage room underneath. The shelves are heavy and it takes
two people to move them.

The entire setup has been painted flat white to match the
walls and ceiling, giving a clean, lively background to the
beautiful flowers and greenery, and providing maximum
light-reflecting surfaces.

THE CARRIÈRE LIGHT-GARDEN

In the Carrière apartment, we tried an experiment with even greater flexibility. Having some pegboard left over from a partitioning job we did in our office, we bought a couple more sheets of pegboard and some one-by-two lumber for framing. When we got these materials put together, with plywood on top and bottom, we thought we'd goofed. It looked like a tremendous unwieldy box, with three sides of the frame encased in pegboard, and a solid plywood top and bottom. But we set it up in a corner that could accommodate a cabinet almost forty-two inches wide and two-and-a-half feet deep, and went to work to make it attractive with paint, Con-tact, and wallpaper.

The first step was to fasten a two-tube fixture into the top, on the inside of the cabinet. Then we built a shelf of plywood, fastened a three-tube fixture under it, and got out our pegboard hooks. With screw-eyes fastened into the ends of the shelf, we found that the shelf with fixture attached could be moved readily by one person who was then recovering from the flu, and we added a series of little shelves from leftover plywood, that can be moved to any location by means of the pegboard shelf-supports, on the back or on either side.

We painted the inside of the cabinet top, walls, and the shelf with flat white to serve as reflector. We had left a little space on either side of the back panel, so that light cords could be carried out inconspicuously to the extension cord connecting with a light socket. And the rest was merely decoration—finishing touches of molding, and a pair of bifold doors on the front to keep the cats from eating all the little green shoots. Because the cabinet is angled across a corner opposite the major seating area of the room, we added a window shade inside the doors, which can be pulled down to shield viewing eyes and the television screen from the lights and their reflections.

These two gardens—the Johnston garden where furniture

was adapted for the base, and the all-new structure of the Carrière garden—averaged about fifteen dollars in cost of building materials, aside from the lighting fixtures. Actually, we did it this way not because it was cheap, but because we wanted to fit our gardens into the space we have available. We could have spent much more money and time by adapting more elaborate furniture to our spaces.

WHEN NOT TO HAVE A LIGHT-GARDEN:

If you want to grow only gesneriads, and have windows with adequate filtered sunlight, an artificial light-garden may be an unnecessary luxury. Begonias also do well on window sills, if you put them in a south window in winter, east in summer. Lots of people have successfully grown flowering plants under incandescent reading lamps, placing the plants where they are not burned by the heat of the bulb, and giving enough water in the surrounding atmosphere to make up for what the lamp takes.

Nevertheless, professional experiment indicates that increasing the light exposure of gesneriads increases their bloom in direct proportion. An increase from six to eighteen hours of light almost tripled the number of flowers. So light-gardening has its merits even for plants that *will* bloom without it. For those specialty plants that are not so adaptable as gesneriads, the light-garden is a real boon.

If you want to grow nothing but philodendrons, which are jungle natives and therefore accustomed to tree-filtered light, a light-garden is unnecessary. But it won't harm them, and when philodendrons are placed in corners of the light-garden, to receive only peripheral light, they add attractiveness to the over-all picture as accents for the light-loving, blossoming plants. Finally, a light-garden is only a plant cemetery unless you give the other requirements—suitable temperature, humidity, and food—so don't grow plants indoors unless you are prepared to give them the tender, loving care they require.

4

Designing with
Light-Garden Plants

Avid hobbyists though we are, we do not believe that any hobby should dominate a home unless it is an integral part of the home environment. Plants are increasingly important in the decorator's scheme, but if they are allowed to dominate the room in which they are shown, the net result is a jungle effect that may be a bit overwhelming to the visitor who does not fully share the hobbyist's enthusiasm. For example, our own light-gardens fit into our homes in the following ways.

THE JOHNSTON TREATMENT

The lower level of the Johnston home is divided lengthwise with about thirty feet of Japanese-print draperies in white and flamingo. The entire area is carpeted in soft green and gold. On one side of the draperies is the recreation room, furnished for comfortable living. With the drapery divider opened, there is a picture-window view of the light-garden on the other side.

The stairway from the upper level leads directly into the light-garden half of the lower area, which we call the "flower-display room," with its delightful scent and colorful view. In midwinter we have twenty or more impatiens plants, all in flower—reds, pinks, and tangerine. The colorful coleus with leaves five to six inches long, white narcissus, and pink and lavender hyacinths in full bloom, add up to a riot of winter

Figure 9   Aquarium fish and their oxygenating plants do well under plant-growth lamps. The fish look luminous and the plants thrive. Plant-growth lamps seem to prevent the formation of algae.

color. On another light-garden table are fifteen red, pink and white geraniums, taking turns showing their finery; and a strawberry plant stretches out to meet the adjacent episcia, which has tiny red blooms.

On still another table is our five-year-old Jerusalem cherry, in full bloom. A passion-flower vine and a philodendron are racing their way to the ceiling on opposite poles. Four feet away from the wall-backed garden, we have another set of two tables. Just beyond the lights at one end are two large plants—a *Monstera deliciosa* and a *Philodendron hostatum*. Tapering toward the front of these tables are two birds-of-paradise *(Strelitzia reginae)*.

And completing the picture of our indoor terrace are two tanks of beautiful goldfish, which live in our outdoor pool in the summer and move indoors for the winter. Each tank is supplied with filters, circulating pump, and oxygenating plants, all doing beautifully under lights and accented with African violets and a hanging basket of Golden Showers begonia.

THE CARRIÈRE TREATMENT

The Carrière light-garden, at the outset, was a source of supply for the outdoor garden in the country. But once the frost had nipped our dahlias, and the red and gold leaves had drifted off the maple trees, the city garden took on a new look. Gardening can be a fascinating winter sport, too.

Geraniums, impatiens, and petunias, a tuberous-rooted begonia, and brilliantly colorful coleus, rooted from leaves, form the nucleus of a decorative corner display. Even with the kitten-proof louvered doors closed, the colors can be glimpsed through the open slats. And with the doors open, the light-garden becomes a miniature terrace, which can be arranged and rearranged over and over again.

With the terrace idea in mind, we had covered the floor of the light-garden with "flagstones" made of Con-tact. Having some yardage left over as a result of painstakingly matching the pattern, we had covered a couple of strong cardboard cartons with it. These were the cartons in which the fluorescent tubes had come, and one was somewhat shorter than the other, so they made very effective steps, strong enough to support potted plants, and light enough to be hung on the pegboard if our decorative fancy should dictate it. (Perhaps it is the nature of the impatient gardener to have a restless urge to change the picture frequently.)

Because Con-tact is waterproof, we have had no difficulty in keeping our light-garden clean, even though it is inevitable that water gets spilled sometimes. By overlapping our seams carefully—and of course, mopping up if we spill too much—we have found both the floor and the cardboard plant-supporting steps to be durable and carefree.

Within this highly flexible framework of decorative possibilities, there is almost no limit to what you can do with your light-garden. There is plenty of light for those plants that need it; and there are the relatively unlighted areas that suit the jungle plants—beyond the range of the direct light, both behind the tubes and in the front, as well as at the ends. As we have mentioned, jungle plants actually don't need to be grown under lights, but neither do they refuse to live and add their decorative touch to the garden picture if they are placed on the periphery.

By hanging the movable shelf fairly high in the garden— about twelve inches below the fixed light in the roof—we created a well-proportioned display space below. So the top section is often used as a nursery and sick bay, hidden from view by pulling down the curtain in front of it. Here, any plants that are not looking their best but are worth saving, and little trays of seeds (because we can't resist having "wee ones" of any kind) are placed with an eye to their welfare rather than their decorative contribution. But in the display garden below, we arrange blooming and green plants entirely as we would utilize the dabs of pigment on our palette.

DESIGN PRINCIPLES

The most interesting picture always has a focal point. So one exceptionally eye-catching plant or group of plants is arranged on or just above the floor, either at the center or at one side. A centered focal point creates a balanced, symmetrical design when subordinate plants are arranged properly at both sides. An off-centered focal point makes an asymmetrical (to us, more interesting) design, when a height line is carried up directly from it, and a low, long line moves out an equal distance at the base. It's fun to create these pictures, and not at all difficult, once you get the hang of it.

APPLIED DESIGN

For example, suppose you want to use three geraniums in a group as your focal point, and you want the focal point to create a left-hand triangle—an asymmetrical design. Let's say there are bright red and salmon-colored geraniums. Coleus will echo these colors well, and if all your coleus

Figure 10   An asymmetrical design is more interesting than a symmetrical arrangement, and is as easy to plan. Height is arranged at one side.

plants are big ones, you simply create small ones by nipping off a few tops and repotting the obliging little creatures.

We always keep a good supply of green plants of various kinds, because they are so useful as a foil to colorful blooms. They don't, for the most part, care much whether they are directly under the lights or not, so they are excellent for background placement. In painting the picture around our geranium focal point, then, we would set the geraniums in the left-hand side, directly under the lights, with the red one and one of the salmon-colored elevated a few inches above the door. A third geranium would be raised about the height of its pot *behind* the red one. This begins the triangle, and gives third-dimensional depth to the design, right at the start.

Immediately to the left of the red geranium, on the floor beside it, would go a green plant—perhaps our Ti leaf, which is now about ten inches tall. Tucked in close in the foreground, directly in front of the geraniums and set on the floor, would be some lower green plants—a shallow planter filled with ajuga, to underline the focal point. And leading out toward the right would be little coleus plants in graduated heights, tapering off to a low green line of tiny cactus. Thus the base line of the triangle is established.

The height line is next, and easily created with a tall green plant. We happen to have a zebra plant that would serve this purpose well, and we would place it directly behind the geranium grouping, elevated just enough to hide its container and make the color line continuous and upward-flowing. Larger coleus plants placed behind the small ones, close to the geraniums and on their right, will soften the inner corner of the triangle, and fill it into a pleasant curve.

The asymmetrical design naturally leaves a blank in the upper right-hand corner, but one of our reasons for liking pegboard walls on a light-garden is that we can hang something from any point we choose. By hanging a cascade begonia in the upper right-hand corner of this design, we would fill in the blank without creating a second focal point, or distracting from the lines of the asymmetrical base arrangement.

SYMMETRICAL STYLING

Symmetrical arrangements are easier to create. The focal point is at the center, with the height line also centered, and you merely have to choose plants that are similar in height and coloring to be placed at the sides. Keep it triangular, tapering out at the outer ends of the base line, and be sure to give it depth by putting the tallest lines *behind* the focal point.

In effect, arranging a garden display is exactly like creating a floral arrangement. Only instead of designing with individual blooms of cut flowers, and pieces of cut greenery and branches, you are using entire plants. So you visualize each plant as a line flower, if it's tall and slender; a form flower, if it has an interesting shape; a mass flower if it is loaded with closely clustered blooms; or a trailer (like ivy). Interesting texture is provided by choosing some green plants that have

Figure 11   This symmetrical arrangement creates a triangle, with the plants grouped evenly on each side of the center height line. Strict adherence to the rules of design is a luxury in a two-shelf light-garden, but is delightfully decorative.

smooth, swordlike leaves, and some that have crinkly leaves with serrated edges.

"That's all very fine," you may be objecting, "but what do I do with the plants that don't happen to fit into this particular design?" No problem. Keep plants in individual containers and remove any you don't need. Light-grown plants don't have to stay under the lights all the time. They can live happily as long as a week outside the light-garden. So just give them effective placement around the house, care for them as they need it, and bring them back to the garden when you change your display.

THE SHOW CAN BE CHANGED

You can also do interesting abstract designs, geometricals, and pleasant crescents, especially if you add a few portable lights to your garden equipment. For example, we sawed the top shelf off an old book stand, leaving the supports that raised it above the lower shelf, to serve as legs. With two 15-watt plant-growth tubes installed under the shelf, we created a little table that can be set into the light-garden whenever and wherever we want it. The nine-inch legs allow room for small plants or seedlings set under the lights, and the table top is a support for plants that need to be closer to the lights above than setting them on the floor would allow.

Attractive balancing groups of plants are then added by means of shelves, hanging baskets, and such, at the opposite side. The major thing to remember when setting up your light-garden as a pictorial display is that, as in any design, you need to start out with an idea. We like to sketch out the design first, because it keeps us from adding "just one more pot" and destroying the effect. It's always a temptation to include a plant that is especially beautiful, just because it *is* beautiful, and too often, it contributes nothing but chaos and disorder. Lines should flow, not jump. Colors should blend, not spot. And if the plant adds nothing, just put it somewhere else, out of the picture, where it can be enjoyed for its individual beauty.

SPECIMEN-PLANT DISPLAYS

Specimen plants that are too large for placement directly under lights in the light-garden can have individual light-garden treatment. For example, put your Jerusalem cherry on a small stand with a triple circular fluorescent lamp suspended directly above it, with a reflector over it like a chandelier. A mammoth caladium, citrus tree, or any exceptionally fine specimen plant that requires plenty of light will show off

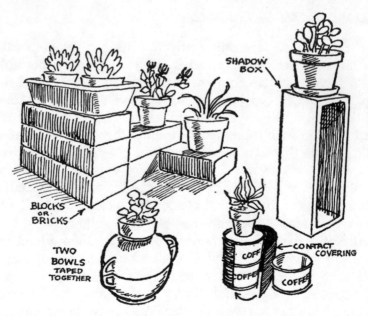

Figure 12   A collection of harmonizing stands makes it easier to relate all of the elements of your light-garden. Bricks can be stacked to raise plants to the desired level. Coffee tins wrapped neatly with Con-tact can be used singly or one atop another. An inverted bowl can be used as a plant support, or two matching bowls can be taped together for added height. And a shadow box can be placed on its end or on its side, according to the height your plants require.

to advantage this way, and become an individual highlight of the room decor.

Those tall plants that normally require partial shade can be set close to the light-garden, where they will receive peripheral light. They'll have to be turned frequently to keep them shapely, since only the side turned toward the garden will be lighted.

POTS AND STANDS

A collection of matching or harmonizing pots or containers makes it easier to relate all the elements of light-garden composition. And interesting stands to raise plants that need to be closer to the light add to the picture, if they are similar.

But if you are a flower-arranging purist, you may feel about containers as you do about flower holders and other mechanics—they should be concealed. One way to do this is to set the pots into large planter boxes, about the same width as the fluorescent fixtures above them, or a little wider. Or attach a molding or apron to the front edge of the shelf to hide the pots and soil. The apron can be made to harmonize with the rest of the room, or to be decoratively attractive in itself. Heavy plastic, metal mesh, formica, or filigree can be used for this purpose.

HANGING BASKETS

Sometimes a nuisance to water, but often worth the trouble to add variety to a decorative indoor garden, is the hanging basket. Ivy geranium, sweet alyssum, fuchsia, browallia, *Campanula isophylla,* oxalis, achimene, episcia, bromeliads and many other trailing and viney house plants do well in baskets hung in the light-garden. Line a rustproof basket with a heavy layer of sphagnum moss. Fill it with rich soil (equal parts of garden loam, leaf mold, topsoil and compost). Firm the soil, arrange the plants, and add more soil if neces-

Figure 13   A hanging basket, with circular tubes mounted in the reflector above it, makes a light-garden wherever you want one. Brass
bowls with chain mountings are commercially available for this purpose. You can also use hanging baskets in corners of the light-garden
to add a decorative note and accommodate plants that need little light.

sary. (Or simply use the moss-lined basket as a holder for a
potted plant.) Some plants can grow over the edge, others
through the moss in the sides of the basket. Moisten the soil
thoroughly after planting, then hang the basket in the light-
garden. To water, take the basket down and immerse it in a
pail of water, then let it drip off before putting it back. Fertilize every two weeks or so.

FOR CHILDREN

Youngsters love miniature plants arranged with doll furniture, animal figures, or rocks. Use your imagination for
"props"—that will help them use theirs. For example, coat-
hangers make effective wrought-iron railings, if you have the

patience to work them up. Then you must visualize your plants as trees and shrubs, and group them accordingly.

Aquariums built in as part of the light-garden appeal to both young and not-so-young, and the swimming fish add motion to the plant colors.

Figure 14   An unused aquarium makes an attractive plant-filled terrarium. Fluorescent lights are concealed by the molding nailed to the wooden top.

You can also make an unused aquarium into a plant-filled terrarium. Use a wooden top to hold the tubes and serve as reflector, painting it flat white and fastening the fixtures under it. Add small corner blocks to allow for air circulation under it. In the tank, lay a shallow foundation of pebbles or gravel on the bottom for drainage. Cover it with a sheet of sphagnum moss, green side up. Then add enough soil mixture to accommodate the roots of whatever plants you intend to grow in it. Equal parts of humus, peat moss, topsoil and sand; or a commercial all-purpose planting mixture, will suit most plants, but try to choose plants that have similar growing preferences.

Miniature plants, ground covers and creepers, and some taller ones to create interesting height lines, accented with a bit of moss, a rock, cork, a piece of bark—these are the nuclei for an artistic miniature landscape. Seen under the lavender tone of plant-growth fluorescents, it will be a bit of fairyland to enchant any child. When it's all planted, spray it with a fine mist, but don't flood it.

Some plants, of course, are natural dwarfs, and there are enough of them in sufficient variety so that you can create an entire light-garden of miniature plants. But you don't have to depend on nature for your dwarfs. In chapter 5 we tell you how to grow plants to size.

Alpine flowers, heaths, heathers, and the hybrid dwarf varieties of plants available from the nursery, all lend themselves to lilliputian decorative uses. And miniature roses, increasingly available, can be used for delightful accent pieces, but as yet with somewhat unpredictable response to light-gardening. Roses are essentially outdoor plants, and have always been considered by rose growers to do best outdoors. We are now embarked on an experiment with miniature roses in our light-gardens, and will report the results when we've reached justifiable conclusions.

So just because you don't have an acre of lush sandy loam is no reason why you cannot have a real show-off garden, right in your city home. You can create, in any room in any house, a living picture composed of growing plants. It can be symmetrical, asymmetrical, formal, informal, or purely unplanned. (We prefer "unplanned" to "untidy.") It can and should reflect *your* personality and *your* interests, just as your furniture and decorative touches reflect you.

As a rule-of-thumb in light-gardening, start with the space that's available for light-gardening equipment that is presently on the market. Then plant what you want to grow, choosing normal-sized plants that will grow to a mature height that fits under your lights, or dwarfing your plants by means of chemicals, root pruning, or simply cutting back the stems that grow too long.

5

Care and Feeding of Light-Garden Plants

We have discussed plants in terms of the light they need to make them eat, digest, and profit from their food. Now we talk about the food itself, the air that plants breathe, and routine maintenance.

GROWING MEDIA

The disintegration of rock and organic matter makes soil. If you have an outdoor garden, you'll want to make a compost pile of the grass cuttings, leaves, and assorted garden refuse that can be disintegrated easily by adding a compost-inducing chemical, readily buyable. A gallon of compost will fill about twenty-five 3-inch or 4-inch pots. If you don't have a compost pile, it's best to buy the packaged planting-soil mixes that are specified for the plants you want to grow, or mixes recommended for house plants in general. For example, if you are planning to grow evergreens such as azaleas, which do exceptionally well in a light-garden, you need a soil mix that is designed for evergreens—more acid than alkaline.

Essential to good soil for plant growth are humus (decayed organic matter) to provide enough live bacteria to assist the plant in digesting its food; sufficient clay to bind the soil together; and sand enough to allow the air and water to move through the clay.

Plants vary in their requirements for water around their roots. Some prefer a sandy soil to give them plenty of drainage, and some want the soil moist at all times. The more sand the soil contains, the greater will be the volume of water that can flow through it without accumulating. The more clay and humus, the greater the accumulation of water around the root system. Roots that cannot use all the water that is available may suffer from root rot. Water-loving plants can use the water, but landlubbers may drown.

Soils are never ideal in nature. Plants that survive natural growing conditions do so because they are able to adapt themselves to adversity, such as too much moisture, too little drainage, too much acidity or alkalinity. So you can rest assured that any soil you concoct especially for a specific plant's needs will be the best soil it ever lived in. By mixing your own growing media tailored to the requirements of your plants, you grow better plants than nature is likely to grow.

Peat moss, perlite, and vermiculite are processed materials. Peat moss is processed from decayed peat that is sterilized, and it can be substituted for compost. Perlite and vermiculite are processed from volcanic residue. All are commercially available in many grades, and can be used either as soil substitutes or as soil additives.

Half vermiculite and half peat moss is another popular mixture for plant growth, in which the vermiculite takes the place of sand, and the peat moss does the job of the loam. There is no nutrition in these sterile, processed materials, and plants that are grown in them must be fed with appropriate plant foods.

There is experimental fun to be had in stirring up your own combinations of natural and processed materials, to create just the mixture that is tailored for your plants. One that we are presently using in our Point Pleasant light-garden is one-fifth cocoa-bean hulls and four-fifths peat moss, substituted for the full portion of peat moss, in any combination of peat moss with vermiculite, perlite, or sand. Best rule of thumb we have heard on the subject of growing media is "if you find one you like, stick to it."

ALL-PURPOSE SOIL

Good for most potted plants is this soil mixture:
   3 parts loam (aged silt and clay)
   1 part peat moss or leaf mold
   1 part builder's sand (this differs from natural sand in that it has been washed until all residue of clays and salts have been washed away). You can make adjustments to this mixture as and if you begin to specialize: For example, for growing cacti and succulents, aim for a highly porous soil with more sand. A quarter cup of bonemeal to a gallon of soil mixture is agreeable to most plants.

SOIL FOR AIR PLANTS

Orchids, bromeliads and other air plants that need a light growing medium around their roots will grow in a mixture of peat moss, perlite, and ground charcoal, with no clay at all—actually no soil. Most professional orchidists use osmunda fibers.

AERATED SWEET SOIL

Even the new gardener can learn to recognize a good soil mixture by the way it feels and smells. It should crumble in the hand yet seem able to retain moisture. Sticky soil will cake and pack down on the roots. Once the plant is potted, you can keep the top soil aerated by digging *gently* into the surface with a small plastic fork, so that air and moisture can enter. Do not injure tender roots. If drainage is good (see page 95) and the holes kept open, the soil should stay sweet for years.

If you are gardening in the city where grime and grease can collect at the surface, occasionally remove the top inch or so of soil and replace it with a fresh soil mixture.

MEDIUM FOR STARTING SEED

We use only a fine grade of vermiculite for starting seed because the roots don't cling to it when you want to transplant, and therefore, there is no transplant shock. Even plants that resent transplanting, and whose seeds are labeled "sow where you want them to grow" can be started in vermiculite and later set where you want them in the soil. This is one of the factors of light-gardening that brings your outdoor garden into earlier bloom. Peat moss, as a seed starter, has given us some trouble, but never vermiculite. Milled sphagnum moss is also an excellent medium in which to start seeds.

HOW TO RE-USE SOIL

Often we find ourselves in need of potting soil with nothing but old soil on hand, in containers that previously held plants that were either transplanted to the outdoor garden or failed to live to maturity. There may be latent disease germs in this soil, especially if the previous plants died; or there may be latent seeds that could still germinate if they were watered. So we learned the hard way, through experience, that before we plant in old soil we must sterilize it. Sterilizing the soil kills both seeds and bacteria, including the living organisms that are good for plant growth, so plants grown in sterilized soil, as in artificial mediums, will need to be fed regularly.

It is now our practice to save our used soil until there is enough to make a sterilizing job worthwhile. Then we put it all into a roasting pan; soak it with water until, as we squeeze it, the water bubbles through the mixture; and then bake it at 200° F. for two hours. When it cakes on top, it's finished. When it has thoroughly cooled, it is ready to use, and can be stored against a time of emergency when we're glad we have it on hand.

PLANTS NEED FERTILIZER

Plants need food. We prefer soluble fertilizers for light-garden plants. There are many different kinds on the market—tablets, dry powder, and liquid. Usually, the fertilizer should be 5-10-5 or 10-6-4 (the first figure always indicates the proportion of nitrogen; the second is phosphorous; and the third, potassium). These proportions are always printed on the labels, along with a listing of the trace elements found in the plant-food mixture. *Do* read these labels carefully and choose a well-balanced plant food that will provide what *your* plants need.

All plants need calcium, even those that are acid-loving, because calcium is a basic plant food. It is provided by lime. Charcoal is a water-sweetener that keeps the water fresh and actively flowing through the plant cells, by retarding the decay of organisms. And iron is one of the most important minor elements for healthful plant growth. These are "trace elements" that should be included in the list on your plant-food label. Extra acidity for plants that need it is provided by sulphur.

Let the plants get fairly dry before you feed them so that they will take into the soil as much food as they can use. With the extra stimulation of light, they are not likely to overfeed —they simply draw on the food supply in the soil as they need it. Light makes them work harder, using more energy, and they must be fed regularly. Either give them a light nutrient (one-eighth to one-quarter of the application directed on the package) at every watering, once they have their full set of leaves; or give them a stronger (full-dose) application every ten days, with sufficient plain water between feedings to keep stems and foliage firm.

WATERING

Study the needs of your individual plants, letting them (and Part II) guide you in how often to water. Check them daily. Overwatering kills more plants than drought, but some plants, like coleus, are thirstier than others, such as geraniums. Let the surface of the growing medium tell you by its feeling of dryness that it's time to water again. When you water, keep the spout close to the soil and pour slowly. This prevents root disturbances and injury to lower stems. And always give them room-temperature water.

Nothing makes you feel more like an expert than tapping the pot to tell if it is dry; but this old-fashioned system works only with some clay pots. If you hear a hollow sound in a clay pot, watering may be necessary; if you hear a dull, heavy thud, the soil is probably moist enough. Pots made of plastic, glazed ceramic, peat, glass, or materials other than natural clay don't talk this language.

The temperature and humidity that are peculiar to your own light-garden will also have their influence on the watering requirements of individual plants. In a light-garden, especially for plants getting maximum light, you need more water than for window-sill plants, because the light keeps the plants continuously active. So choose a growing medium that holds moisture, but does not compact too much around the plant roots. Vermiculite and perlite hold moisture and are therefore good growing mediums. In natural potting soils, the proportion of clay should not be too great.

If your light-garden is on a cool porch, water plants sparingly in winter, and only early in the day. (In a cold room, we would be tempted to suggest plugging in a 25-watt incandescent lamp to the fluorescent setup, for the warmth it would bring. Keep it about twelve inches above the nearest leaf.)

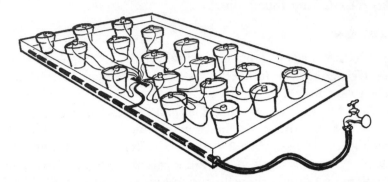

Figure 15 Commercially available automatic watering devices feed water to each pot by means of individual hoses connected to a master hose. An automatic timer can be added to turn the water on and off and also to turn the lights on and off.

For light-gardeners who take extensive vacations, automatic watering devices are as important as automatic timers that turn the lights on and off according to schedule. There are systems of little hoses that stem from a master hose hooked to a faucet, supplying each plant with water at the times arranged by the automatic timer setting. Or you can provide a home-made system *without* automatic timing by means of wicking.

Wicking comes in balls and is available at hardware stores. By cutting it into whatever lengths you need to reach from a dishpan of water placed near the plants, you can supply each pot with its own individual siphon, merely by keeping one end of the wick in the water pan, and the other anchored in the soil of the pot. The wicks will dry out if sun reaches them in the midriff; the system works best if it is set up where no sun can reach. One dishpan filled with water should take care of two dozen medium-sized pots for about two weeks.

CIRCULATING MOIST AIR

The atmosphere plants breathe and live in determines whether or not they will survive. Plants must have at least 30 percent relative humidity, and do better at 50 percent. They can enjoy up to 70 percent, but neither people nor furniture can be sacrificed to the needs of humidity-loving plants that belong in a greenhouse rather than a living room. Most plants can take drier conditions.

Humidity gauges indicate relative humidity. Some of them are combined with thermometers. The inexpensive types, readily available wherever you buy thermometers and also in most seed catalogues, are satisfactory for light-garden purposes. But if *your* healthy skin, nose, and throat feel dry, you can be certain that the air in your home is too dry for your plants, even if you don't have a humidity gauge.

If your furnace is equipped with a humidifier, humidity and air are automatically controlled in your living atmosphere, which you share with your light-garden plants. If you have no automatic control over the humidity and air circulation, you can arrange it in these ways:

Set your plants on rimmed trays or baking tins filled with quarter-inch builder's gravel. Keep the trays watered to a point just below the tops of the stones, and set the plants over them. As the water evaporates, the resulting humidity centers around the plants. Air loses its humidity rapidly as it moves away from plants, and this makes it possible to grow desert plants on the same shelf with those that need normal humidity. We set our lantana, for example, directly on the gravel in the humidity tray. A foot or more away on the same shelf, cacti and succulents will grow happily without drainage saucers.

Air circulation may be provided in a light-garden at the time it is built, as we described in chapter 3. Don't be afraid to open the windows on pleasant days, even in cold weather, but avoid drafts caused by opening windows directly opposite the plants on both sides. Basement gardens especially need the open-window ventilation.

TEMPERATURE

Plants will adjust to a temperature up to 70° or 75° F. during the day or when the lights are on; and to night temperatures between 60° and 65° F. A good many plants will adjust to greater extremes. You can find a wide range that will grow at 10° more or less than the ideals given, provided they do not have to make too sudden an adjustment.

Temperature plays an important role in plant growth. It influences the rate of absorption by the roots, transpiration, respiration, assimilation of carbon dioxide, and production of chlorophyll. There is a direct relationship between temperature and light. The more intense the light is, the higher the temperature, so light intensity can be made to compensate for low temperatures when plants are not in an ideal climate.

Conversely, during the dark period, cool temperatures aid the plants in assimilating their food, which is manufactured during the light period. To help you maintain the optimum temperatures for your plants, an accurate thermometer is a light-garden must.

If you have no storm windows and your light-garden is located near a window when the temperature drops suddenly, protect the plants by stuffing paper, cloth or other insulating material around the cracks of the windows to keep the drafts out.

SPACING THE PLANTS

Wherever your light-garden is located, and whatever its construction, always place the individual plants far enough apart so that air can circulate around their containers as well as their foliage. Crowding results in weak stems and provides ideal conditions for pest and disease growth. In general, see

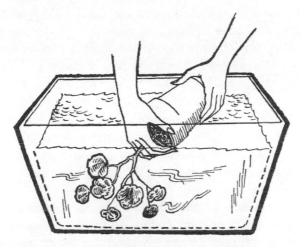

Figure 16 Dunking an infested plant in a tubful of lukewarm water drowns the pests and dissolves dust that may have accumulated on the foliage. It is safer for the plant than a shower bath.

to it that the leaves of one plant don't touch those of another.

CONTROLLING PESTS AND DISEASES

Insecticides are not usually necessary in light-gardens, but occasionally you may bring in a plant that comes complete with a plant pest, or that attracts one through your open windows. Cyclamen mites, red spider mites, and mealy bugs are the vicious three that might attack your well-guarded light-garden plants. You can control them with prepared insecticides in spray cans, but be sure to read the instructions before you buy them. Tropical fish, pet animals and birds, and people may be seriously injured by breathing these insecticides in a closed room. Because we are always well equipped with animals and children, we prefer the safer treatment of a quick bath for infested house plants.

We dunk them for a half minute or less in a tubful of lukewarm water (not more than 90° F.), which drowns the pests and also dissolves any dust that may have accumulated on the foliage. You have to hold your hand over the soil in the pot, and simply submerge the entire plant in the water. (The force of a shower could knock the plants down and perhaps break their stems, and it would not reach the undersides of the leaves, so a shower is not the appropriate bath for plants.) Those with delicate blooms should not be bathed until the blooms are gone, unless the pest is more prolific than the flowers, in which case you have much to lose by waiting. In the average home, with reasonable care, there will never be such a problem.

If your plants are suffering from a fungus disease and have developed brown spots and disfigured forms, the safest thing to do is to cut off the diseased parts, burn them, and let the roots produce new, healthy shoots. If the disease is too far advanced for a pruning job to clean up the mess, you'll save the rest of your garden by throwing out the entire plant. Of course, you'll want to try to save your rare plants, but if severe pruning doesn't do the trick, buy another, healthier plant.

PLANT QUARANTINE

Preventive treatment practiced by all commercial growers and many serious amateurs is to provide a quarantine area where newcomers to the plant family may be observed for three weeks or so, to be certain that they are as healthy as the established local residents. If you have no isolation ward, put the probationer on the shelf with the others, but cover it with a clear plastic bag, pulled down over the plant like a slip cover. Keep it covered until you are sure it's healthy.

PRUNING—WHY AND WHEN

Pruning leaves and stems above the soil level is done to improve the shape of a leggy plant, or to increase the family by providing cuttings. Coleus, for example, can take fairly frequent trimming. When it gets too tall to be attractive, nip off the top shoots, and it will send out new ones at the sides —and vice versa, when it gets too bushy. Root the cuttings and start new plants from them. (Perhaps pruning is too drastic a term. If you trim and pinch off the tips of plants while they are young and soft, the plants stay symmetrical and you avoid real pruning later.)

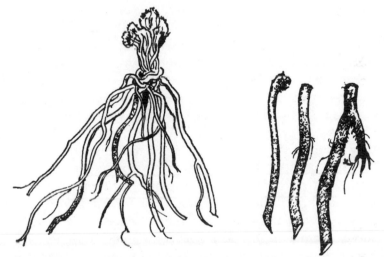

Figure 17 Root pruning is done primarily in bonsai, but is a method for keeping plants dwarfed to fit comfortably into your light-garden.

Root pruning is not often necessary, and is done primarily in bonsai, a special hobby that pertains mostly to outdoor plants. For indoor plants, chemical dwarfing is more practicable and easier. But if you want to keep your plants dwarfed by root pruning, let them get quite dry, shake off the soil from the roots, and cut the major roots almost as short as the top growth. Return the plant to the same pot it had been in.

Roots and tops normally tend to balance and maintain

about the same length. If roots fail to develop soon enough to keep pace with top growth, pinch back the top growth so that the roots will strengthen and lengthen.

GROWING PLANTS TO SIZE

If you are inclined to experiment, you'll be intrigued with the possibilities of dwarfing plants with chemicals. There are several chemicals now available at your garden center that, when used according to directions, will make your plants grow shorter stems yet produce normal-sized blooms and foliage. Phosphon and CCC are dwarfing chemicals that are added to the soil in which the plants grow. They are effective for one year, keeping the distance between nodes about half as long as normal. To repeat or continue the dwarfing process, more of the chemical must be added each year.

In 1963 a spray-on dwarfing chemical was developed. At this writing, it is still in the testing stages; but we have seen an entire garden at Burpee Seed Company's experimental farm that was literally sprayed to size. Charming miniature plants comprised the garden, and their height was controlled entirely by the amount of dwarfing chemical that had been sprayed onto foliage and stems. It is now available on the market under the name B-9, labeled for experimental use.

KEEPING ANNUALS IN BLOOM

As soon as annuals have finished flowering, they put all their energy into seed-making. To keep annuals flowering, pinch off the dead flowers before seeds form.

DO PLANTS NEED REPOTTING?

Roots don't usually want to see or be seen. They prefer darkness because their food is in the dark soil. If roots cannot go down deep into bottomless soil, they spread out horizontally, for it is their job to find food to nourish greenery and blossoms, and they are dedicated to it.

A plant that is valued primarily for its blooms or fruits rather than its foliage should usually be kept potbound. This means that the roots are tightly confined. Potbound plants often produce more blooms than those whose roots have plenty of room for growth.

When a plant has been in its pot long enough so that it is mature and not continuing to grow, it is well to take it out carefully and see if it needs repotting. Water the plant well, allowing it to absorb all the moisture it will take. Drain it, and when the soil is just moist lift the soil ball from the pot. If the roots are crowded, but alive and healthy looking, place the soil ball in a pot that is one size larger than the one from

Figure 18   Blooming and fruiting are increased by keeping the plant potbound, but when the plant loses its healthy look, remove it from the pot and check the soil ball. It's time to repot if the roots are crowded like this.

which you took it, fill in with fresh soil, and leave it alone. If there are dead roots and lots of new baby rootlets, with room for growth once the dead roots are cut out, prune both new roots and dead ones, and repot in the original pot from which you took it.

HARDENING OFF

If you are planning to move your plants outdoors from your light-garden, you should get them ready to accept the change before you leave them to fend off the elements by themselves.

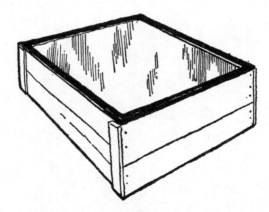

Figure 19   A cold frame is excellent for the hardening off period when plants are made ready for a move from the light-garden to the outdoor garden.

Under lights, they have been pampered with ideal conditions to the point of being extremely delicate.

The first move to the outdoor garden should be from the light-garden to an unheated, wind-sheltered spot in which they can harden without suffering a traumatic experience. A protected porch, a sun room, a cold frame—all are good. Glass, hard plastic, or soft plastic can provide the shelter from night winds and big daytime gusts during this transition period. The plants can be exposed to soft breezes during the day, but must be sealed against night winds.

Two to three weeks in this sheltered environment should harden them sufficiently so that they can be set out into the outdoor garden. But be prepared to cover them all with sheets of soft plastic, or to bring them indoors, if a sudden below-freezing temperature is predicted. If you are a weekend gardener, better keep the plants where you can get at them until the weather is guaranteed to be balmy. Lightweight plastic containers make these moves easier.

Those plants that bloom right up until the really heavy frost begins, and those that start early in the season to produce flowers and leaves, can withstand a quick transition from indoors to out. They adjust readily to temperature changes. But just in case there's a late frost, keep a few of your favorite plants remaining under the lights to serve as replacements if necessary.

BRINGING PLANTS INDOORS

When summer is over, many of your blooming plants can be brought indoors to continue blooming under lights for a longer period. They do not need any conditioning or transition period, if you give them their preferred humidity. It's better to bring them in before there is likelihood of frost, because the first frost almost inevitably catches you in your shorts.

There is no special trick to this move if you have decided

in advance of outdoor planting that you are going to bring them in at the end of the season. In this case, plant them outdoors in their pots, so that they are easier to lift out of the garden. But some of the so-called annuals, usually labeled "hardy annual" or "half-hardy", can be treated as perennials if you take them out of the outdoor climate that would frost-kill them, and keep them under lights until the following summer. These plants, having started small, would have outgrown their pots by the end of summer, and perhaps were started in peat pots that have disintegrated into the soil. So dig as widely as possible around the root system, as deep as necessary to avoid breaking major roots, and transfer the root ball with the soil it has been growing in directly into a waiting pot that can be set into the light-garden.

Among these so-called annuals that are actually tender perennials are petunias and impatiens, and of course, geraniums. We always set our geraniums outdoors in their pots, but the petunias and impatiens grow too much during the summer season to be set out as potted small plants. How long their bloom can be extended is difficult to predict with certainty, but fun for experiment. Geraniums will need a complete rest. Impatiens almost never stops blooming. For over two years we have kept impatiens in almost constant bloom indoors and out.

Sometimes it's better to discard the plant after its first season, and take cuttings to be rooted, rather than to try to bring the whole plant into the light-garden. Coleus and geraniums can be grown successfully from year to year, but the older they get, the more coarse in texture and grotesque in shape they are likely to become, even though perfectly healthy. They are then oddities, rather than beauties in the prime of life, and cuttings are better.

FLOWER-SHOW TRANSPORTATION

These moves from light-garden to outdoors and back again

cut stems
here

Figure 20   Geraniums can be carried over from year to year, but when they become coarse in texture and leggy, it's time to prune them back, discard woody sections of the stem, and root the cuttings. New shoots will appear from the roots of the old plant.

are scheduled for warm weather. But the flower show in which you want to enter your light-grown plant may occur in cold weather, and transporting the plant safely will take special care. One of the advantages of expanded polystyrene plant containers is their insulating quality, so we like them as slip-covers for pots that have to be transported in winter. But lacking this convenience, the safest method is to use two cardboard cartons, one nested in a larger one, with crumpled newspaper or vermiculite between them. Setting the plants into the smaller carton, pack more crumpled newspaper or vermiculite around the pots, and cover the entire carton with several layers of folded newspaper over the top, securely tied around the sides so that no cold air can get to the plants. Then, even if it's only a short walk, warm up the car with the heater on, and chauffeur the plants to the exhibit area with a minimum of outdoor exposure.

HOSPITALIZATION AND VACATION

If your plants seem about to die, it's really best to get them out of your garden. But if you can't bear to give them up, lights can do much for sick plants that have any life left in them. And sometimes all they need is some extra iron, which is now available in a fast-release iron source that can bring them back to normal almost overnight.

In Part II we have indicated those indoor plants that go dormant and need a complete rest. Since light keeps them active, the plants that need a vacation should be removed from the light-garden and allowed to rest in a cool, dark place before they are returned to the light.

BULBS

Most bulbs that can be forced indoors are not at all fussy about the hours of light they get. They seem to do as well with ten hours of daily light as with sixteen. We keep them in the end-zones of the light-garden after the green shoots show only to speed blooms, moving them up to our kitchen or dining table when they begin to flower. The lights accelerate flowering time. If you need blossoms for a special occasion, put bulb pots under off-center lights about four or five days before the event. As soon as bulbs flower, move them upstairs or give them end-zone light, since intense light will fade the flowers.

All spring-flowering bulbs need a cool rooting period. If you want to delay flowering time, keep the bulb pots in a cool dark place. Remember that warmth is as much a factor as light in causing bulbs to bloom, after they have had their cool rooting period. If you live in an apartment, you are probably better off buying bulbs that have been planted. You will have the fun of seeing the flower develop, without the task of planting. However, Win Carrière gives potted bulbs a month in the apartment refrigerator at 40° F. to replace the normal three-month outdoor winter. They bloom two months earlier.

POTTING BULBS

If you buy imported bulbs, plant them as soon as possible in a flower pot with good drainage. Put pieces of broken flower pot, charcoal, or pebbles in the bottom of the pot. Add an all-purpose soil so that the pot is two-thirds full. Now put in the bulbs, closely spaced but not touching. Top with a thin layer of soil, so that the nose of the bulb is barely covered. Firm the soil by pressing down gently with your fingertips. Water well and label the pots.

To develop the root system, the bulbs should now be stored in a cool dark cellar (about 40° F.) or in a trench in wooden boxes or bushel baskets covered with peat moss. If you will stagger the plantings, you can have somewhat continuous bloom from November through March.

After the root system is established, you can gradually bring the bulbs into the light. Put them in a shaded cool place for about a week, until the pale shoots turn greener. Then move them into the light-garden, placing them under the ends of the fluorescent tubes. With moderate light and warmth, they should bloom in two to four weeks, depending on their varieties. It is at this point that you can speed or delay their blooming time by giving them more or less light and warmth. Keep the humidity level up, and when they begin to flower, take them out from under the lights or move them into a corner of the light-garden where the light is only peripheral.

Cut off dead flowers, and don't put the bulbs into darkness

until the leaves have begun to turn brown. Then take them out of their pots, dry them off, and store them in a cool dark place again. They cannot be forced a second time indoors, but they can be planted outdoors and will flower there.

Bulb catalogs list many varieties that can be forced well indoors, and hyacinths, daffodils, tulips (single and Darwin), crocuses, and muscari are all reliable.

6

Increasing the Family

Plants can be propagated from seed from transplanted seedlings, by cuttings, or by division. Regardless of how you increase your plants, their root systems all react in a protective manner. Roots bury themselves in the soil, furrowing for food and, in general, try to balance the length of their above-ground stalks with similar length.

GROWING FROM SEED

Whether seeds germinate faster in darkness or in light is as yet unknown. To find the answer, the Burpee Seed Company set up an experimental light-garden, planting seeds of parsley and verbena; seedlings of asters, pertunias, etc.; and cuttings of African violets, geraniums, and chrysanthemums. Their experiment was minimal, and they believed that results were not sufficiently encouraging to warrant further tests with seed germination under light. Burpee did conclude that cuttings showed marked improvement under lights, and that seedlings grew more vigorously.

Experiments at Beltsville seem to indicate that light *may* speed germination, but a decade or more may pass before results are conclusive.

Meanwhile, Arno and Irene Nehrling, in *A Picture Book of*

Perennials just off the press, state that *achillea, centranthrus, thyme, valeriana,* and some *violas* actually require sun to start germination.

Our own practice is a compromise with the established method. We plant seeds in thoroughly moistened vermiculite or milled sphagnum moss, in market packs or deep aluminum frozen-food trays, cover with polyethylene bags to keep the moisture in, then with newspaper to keep the light out.

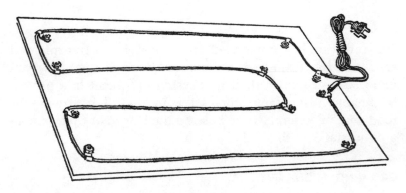

Figure 21   A thin sheet of Styrofoam with an insulated heating cable attached is what we use in the Carrière garden for providing bottom heat to speed seed germination. We turn it on for about eight hours, and off for the remaining sixteen each day until the seeds sprout.

We give them about eight hours of bottom heat with a heating cable or by placing them on top of the electric hot-water heater or on a shelf warmed by the light-garden fluorescents under it. The growing medium is thus heated to 75° to 85° F. Then we subject them to sixteen hours without bottom heat (60° to 70° F.) unless they are tropical plants, which need only eight or ten hours at this lower temperature. If the seeds haven't germinated in an appropriate time, we remove the newspaper and put the containers, still in their plastic bags, under the lights until sprouts show. They must be kept moist with a spray of water but not flooded.

In general, small seeds are planted shallowly, and very fine seed may have to be mixed with sand, sown over the surface of the growing medium without a covering layer, and misted into position. Seeds of plants that do not like to be transplanted are sown directly into strips of peat pots. In each 1-inch peat pot, we sow about six small seeds; or four medium-sized seeds; or two large ones. When they sprout, we thin them out easily, since their roots do not cling to vermiculite.

Planting depth depends on the size of the seed. If they are large enough to be seen readily, they need to be covered with growing medium to about twice the size of the seed. Hard-coated seeds must be soaked overnight in tepid water

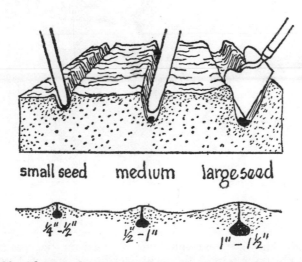

small seed   medium   large seed

¼"-½"   ½"-1"   1"-1½"

Figure 22   Planting depth depends on the size of the seed. Tiny seeds should be pressed into the growing medium surface, firmed into place, and given a light misting of water without covering. Other seeds that are large enough to be covered should be planted like this.

before they are planted. This softens the coat, allowing water
and oxygen to enter the seed.

Unless the seedlings are pricked off into a soil mixture
before they are one inch tall, they must be given a light nutrient. We always prefer liquid plant fertilizers, or powders

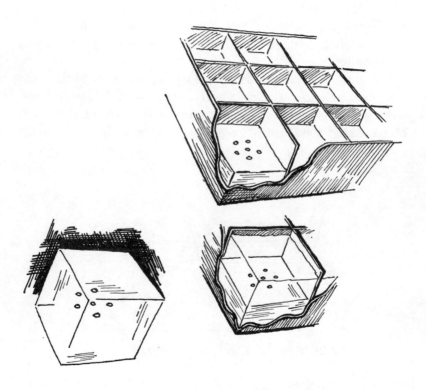

Figure 23   There's experimental fun in stratifying biennial seeds in
your ice-cube tray, to see if they will bloom the first year. Freeze half
a trayful of water, scatter the seeds on the ice, very gently pour in
more water to fill the tray, and freeze for about a month. Sometimes
the plants will react as though they had had an entire winter, and
bloom the first year.

that can be dissolved readily, and feed the plants with every watering, using about one-eighth of the full-strength dose recommended on the package.

WHY SEEDS FAIL TO GERMINATE

Although commercially packaged seeds are usually very dependable, with a good percentage of germination, home-grown seeds may prove disappointing. We have patiently waited for sprouts to show, watering and pampering hopefully, and finally given up in despair because not a whisker of green appeared.

Sometimes this failure is because we buried the seeds too deeply. Sometimes it's because the growing medium was too wet or too cold. We use a fine mist sprayer to water newly planted seeds as well as tender little newly sprouted seedlings. Too much water in the growing medium will displace the seeds—they'll float out of position—and drown them too. We always thoroughly moisten and drain the vermiculite in which we start most of our seeds, before we plant the seeds in it. Thus moistened, the vermiculite will draw water into itself when its dry surface indicates that it's time for another sprinkling. And of course, you can prevent the seeds from catching cold by giving them bottom heat to warm the growing medium.

SEEDLINGS

Seedlings need to be grown close to the light or they will become leggy. We keep the light-loving ones only a few inches below the tubes, under the most effective center portion. As they grow taller, we lower them, keeping them still under the center of the tubes. If they require less intense light when they are mature, we start them in their preferred position under the ends of the tubes where the light has less energy.

Figure 24   African violet leaves can be rooted in water or vermiculite. Make a little collar of cardboard to cover the container, slit it so that the leaf stem can be inserted, and watch the roots form below the supported leaf.

HOW TO TAKE CUTTINGS

When plants get too big, they can be snipped off at the crown and rooted. This method is particularly effective with African violets and begonias. Cut the stem close to the next cluster that grows below it, so that no stem is left to rise above a blooming or potentially blooming cluster of leaves, and you'll have two plants instead of one.

Similarly, when plants get leggy or too bushy to be attractive, as we mentioned under pruning, choose the best of the shoots that you have pruned off, and start new plants from

Figure 25   Rex begonia and gloxinia leaves can be pinned to a growing medium with slits cut across their veins, and roots will form where
the slits have been made.

them. Some, such as coleus and African violets, will root from
a single leaf if you merely put the stem in water or soil. Others
need more time, and a rooting compound to help them get
started. Rex begonia and gloxinia leaves can be pinned to a
rooting medium if you slit the leaf and pin it in several places.
Roots will come from the slits. A cutting is usually taken at
an angle with a sharp knife, just below a joint or "node" in
the stem (the point of insertion of a leaf), with not more than
a quarter-inch of stem. Dip the cut stem into a hormone
powder for quick rooting, plant it in any sterile growing
medium such as vermiculite or perlite, and a few days later

Figure 26   A cutting is usually taken at an angle with a sharp knife, just below a node, leaving about a quarter inch of stem.

it will usually show roots. Then you can transplant it to a growing medium in an appropriate pot, with or without a light fertilizer. If it is planted in a sterile growing medium, remember to give it regular feedings as described above. A polyethylene tent around a new cutting will keep in the moisture.

As a general rule, all leaves but the top two should be stripped off when you take a cutting. Stick the stem into the soil so that the node below which you made the cut is covered. Vines are the exception to this rule. Virginia creeper, ivies, or strawberry, for example, which grow roots at almost every joint, do not need to have the leaves removed. You can take a long trailer of the vine, bury its cut end in soil, and lightly soil-cover the nodes that have roots or leaves. It will take root in all the expected places and some unexpected ones, wherever it touches the ground. Vines are attractive in

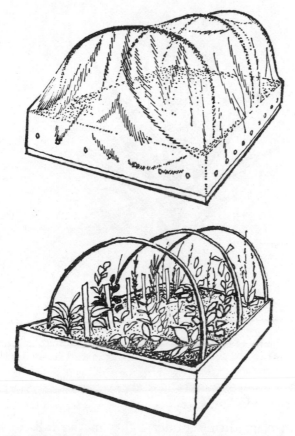

Figure 27 Polyethylene tents are excellent protection for new cuttings while they are taking root. Fill a seed flat with vermiculite, and
bend coat hanger wires above it to form arches. Stretch a sheet of
clear plastic over the wires and tuck the edges under the flat to keep
the moisture in.

the light-garden if you keep them under control by pruning
when necessary. They are usually shade-loving, and therefore can be trained to hang down from one shelf toward another, or to climb up in corners for an interesting accent
around the more sun-loving flowers.

Figure 28   Plants that have a rosette-type leaf formation should be cut an inch or two below the rosette without regard for nodes, leaving the rosette intact.

NEW SHRUBS FROM OLD

We like to start shrubs under lights in the fall, to be set outdoors in spring. We use new growth taken from the tips. Take them similarly to the way you take house-plant cuttings, but where there is a rosette-type leaf formation, as in rhododendrons, azalea, or euonymus, leave the foliage rosette intact, and cut a very short stem—an inch or two below the rosette—without regard for nodes. Stick it into appropriate moistened growing medium, keep it moist at all times, and it should take root.

Holly propagates with difficulty from cuttings, so it's an interesting challenge. Holly cuttings should be new growth, and taken *only* in August or September.

Evergreens with narrow leaves or needles can be cut for propagation in the fall, taking a new growth and cutting at an angle about four inches below the point where the needles or clusters of leaves grow. Dip them into a rooting hormone and keep them with their cut stems in a slightly acid growing medium. A mixture of three parts peat to one part vermiculite or perlite is good. A cold frame will be best for them in the winter. In the spring, they can be put in the light-garden but kept cool for their first summer, and set outdoors in the late summer months. They'll take care of themselves from there on.

Experiments by the U. S. Department of Agriculture indicate that cuttings of many woody plants root faster and more extensively under incandescent light used to extend the normal day length. In some cases, the long-day period stimulated earlier budding and shoot growth. Not all woody plants responded in the same way, but none was injured by the treatment. Beltsville scientists recommend that if you are propagating your woody cuttings *only* under artificial light, with no natural light at all, you combine flourescents and incandescents. They have not conclusively tested rooting under fluorescents, although they do use plant-growth lamps in much of their work.

During the rooting process, cuttings need little or no ventilation, but their growing medium must be kept at about a 70° F. temperature.

DIVISION

Hardy plants, bulbs, corms, rhizomes, and tubers stay in the ground through the winter for two, three, or more seasons, after which you should dig them up and divide them, making more plants and discarding the older parents if they look worn out. Some can be brought in for forcing in the light-garden. Bulbs that are shriveled and dried up will probably not be worth saving. Hardy plants that are not producing enough bloom or are too big for their locations are also ready for division.

Notable among the hardy bulbs are iris, spring-blooming crocuses, daffodils, tulips, hyacinths, and such. Tender bulbs, like gladioli and dahlias, must be taken up and rested over the winter, because they cannot stand soil temperatures below 40° F. yet won't grow at all in the tropics.

Scaled bulbs, such as lily bulbs, reproduce by growing little new bulblets between the scales, which can be picked off and planted. Gladiolus corms, when taken up at the end of the season, will be found to have lots of small bulblets, all of which can be planted and grown under lights until they reach blooming size—almost an inch in diameter. Iris are grown from rhizomes, and so long as they have an inch or two of stem, they will send out roots and leaves, and eventually bloom. Sometimes they will bloom the first year after planting. Dahlias are tubers, and if, when you pull them out of the ground before frost, they have obvious eyes, each eye can become a new dahlia. All of these babies, if grown under lights, will develop faster. They need a couple of months of rest, but not a whole winter. The rest should preferably be in a dark, dry place, so that they can come back with full vigor.

Peonies, chrysanthemums, and lily-of-the-valley are examples of plants that are divided simply by driving a spade through the center of the plants, or using a sharp knife to sever them, in order to keep them from spreading all over the map. This treatment is the only way to divide them successfully, because they do not respond well to being dug up and divided above ground. The resultant cuttings can be grown under lights until they outgrow the light-garden.

WHAT TO PLANT IN

Seed flats are fine for large greenhouses and commercial establishments, but even commercial growers are now growing many of their plants in papier mâché market packs. Seed flats have to be lined with foil or plastic to hold the moist soil, and although they come in several sizes, most of them are too large and unattractive for light-garden use.

We grow most of our little plants in market packs, peat-pot strips, or aluminum-foil dishes. These dishes are useful

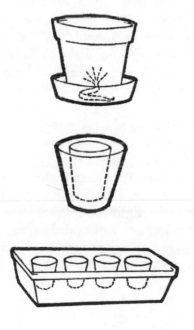

Figure 29   There are several methods of potting plants. The wick-watering pot (top) is good for plants that should not have water on their leaves, since water reaches them through the wick in the bottom from the saucer. Double-potting (center) is a popular method, in which one pot is set inside a larger one, with vermiculite filling the space between. Water is fed into the vermiculite, which covers the smaller pot, and capillary action keeps it circulating. Small pots (below) can be set into a window box, with or without soil around them, to make a neat grouping.

only if they are at least an inch deep, and not too many are, so we collect and prize them.

Paper pots hold too much water in their bottoms, and tend to rot the roots unless the plant is a water-loving variety. When we use them, we always put a layer of charcoal in the bottom. Peat pots are unquestionably preferable, because they can be set into the ground without disturbing the plants in them, and disintegrate completely into the soil. Coffee tins are not bad if you punch a few holes in their bottoms for air and drainage, and use charcoal under the soil. And expanded polystyrene pots are the first real successor to the ever-useful clay pots, because they do everything a clay pot does, but weigh about as much as a breath of air. Hard-plastic pots can be used, and if you can find them in dark colors they are said to absorb heat and create higher soil temperatures to enhance growth, for those plants that want warmth.

Quart milk cartons are always readily available, and lend themselves to temporary use during the seed-sprouting stage. Cut away one side, lengthwise, and fill the resulting box with planting medium. The seedlings, when transplanted into the soil, can go into something more attractive if they are to be displayed in the light-garden.

Self-watering containers are useful especially when seedlings are mature enough to transplant. There are the wick-water types and the pressure types; and in both cases, you don't pour water directly into the soil, but fill the well of the container when it is necessary. The plants take up water as they need it, and the need for refilling is obvious when the well is dry. We have some plastic pressure-watering containers that have kept our plants happily moist for five weeks without refilling, and some wick-watering planters that have to have more water added every four days, because they hold less.

Primarily, you need a container that is deep enough to hold the roots of the plant as long as you want the plant to be in

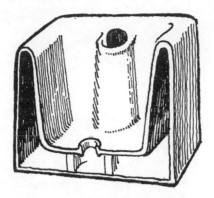

Figure 30   Our favorite pressure-type self-watering container would look like this if we cut it apart. Water is poured into the stoppered hole at the end, filling the well and feeding the roots as they require moisture through a valve in the bottom. We refill ours every five weeks.

the container. So if you intend it to be there permanently, plant in a deep enough container to hold the mature roots, so that you won't have to transplant often. And it needs to have air circulation and water drainage. If there is no provision for drainage, you should add charcoal to keep the soil from souring. Crushed charcoal is advisable, so that it will be distributed and mixed into the soil.

7

Light-Gardening for Profit

There is no reason why light-gardening should not be a source of income, as many other hobbies are. In fact, it is being used now in widely varied ways by flower shops, interior decoration studios, and as a supplement in small-greenhouse operations.

For example, a florist in New York City who rents plants to decorate offices and commercial buildings grows his plants under lights in the basement of his flower shop. Often, when a plant has served its purpose for a customer for a few weeks or months, it comes back to the shop in need of rejuvenation. A visit to the light-garden puts the plant back into rental condition again in short order.

Another New York florist who specializes in terrace plantings has a large light-garden in his shop display area. Many of his customers, intrigued by the idea of light-gardening, have gone into the hobby for themselves under his guidance and instruction. And his display of tropical plants growing under fluorescent lights at the International Flower Show attracted large crowds.

Interior decorators are using plants as freely as fabrics in creating decorative effects, and light-gardens with live plants may take the place of artificial floral materials in city apartments.

Plate I. Against a carved screen, two potted azaleas (in full light), an African violet (in less intense light), and cacti and succulents (in peripheral end light) make a colorful display under the two 20-watt Gro-Lux lamps in a portable light fixture.

Plate III. A portable light-garden set into an unused fireplace makes a
decorative focal point in the living room. A piece of driftwood supported
by the grate adds interest.

Plate II. *(Opposite)* The Carrière light-garden is a
pegboard-walled cabinet, set into a corner of an
apartment living room. The upper shelf is the sick
bay and nursery, where seedlings and dormant plants
are kept under one warm white and one daylight
fluorescent tube. The lower section, whose proportions can be changed by raising or lowering the shelf,
is the display garden. Three 20-watt Gro-Lux tubes
are fastened under the shelf. Small shelves hooked
into the pegboard walls supplement little tables and
Con-tact-covered cartons that raise plants to the desired levels.

Plate IV.   A light-garden setup in a downstairs recreation room utilizes a chain-supported industrial fixture housing two 40-watt Gro-Lux tubes over a sturdy table. A portable light-garden on the tables raises small plants closer to the large fixture and gives added light to flowering azaleas placed below it, under two 20-watt Gro-Lux tubes. Taller plants and plants that need less light intensity are in end zones and on the periphery.

Plate V. A child's garden, set up by seven-year-old Richard Anders inside his toy fort. Consisting largely of small green plants and tiny coleus, with cacti and bromeliads, the plants receive sufficient light from a single Gro-Lux tube in the desk lamp (easily swiveled to give light when needed to an adjoining play surface). Flowering plants would need more light intensity than the 20 watts the desk lamp provides.

Plate VI. Useful in controlling size of plants to limits of light-garden height, Phosfon, one of the new dwarfing chemicals, made the difference in these two chrysanthemums. Potting soil for the one on the right was treated with Phosfon; the one on the left was not treated. Note that the blooms are the same size. The only difference is in the height of the stem, and the bushiness of the foliage.

Plate VII. *(Below)* The Johnston light-garden is built into the lower level of the home, adjacent to a playroom and close to the outdoor garden. Movable shelves and supplementary small tables and stands make it a flexible setup that can be changed frequently. It is constantly in bloom throughout the fall and winter seasons.

Plate VIII.   A utilitarian light-garden for the gesneriad specialist is
created by arranging two double-tube fixtures with Gro-Lux lamps
under each of three shelves supported one above the other with
metal legs. A pulley chain supports the top shelf under two industrial fixtures on legs, making the top section flexible. Note the
use of shelf ends for hanging plants that need little light intensity.

Plate X. *(Above)* Chrysanthemums placed in the end zone close to the light source (horticulturally correct) make the height line of an asymmetrical design. Croton adds color, under the other end zone, and green plants are arranged where they receive little of the light, but add their decorative touches. Driftwood and a carved bird, colorful containers, dried Chinese lanterns, and a flame-like color harmony of yellow, orange, and red make this fireplace grouping a brilliant focal point.

Plate IX. *(Opposite)* A niche in a built-in bookcase makes room for a decorative little light-garden. With the adjustable roof of the portable light-garden raised as high as possible, there is exactly the right light provision for a potted mum directly under the end of the two 20-watt Gro-Lux tubes. A colorful croton occupies the other end, and an azalea and two African violets are set in the foreground. Green plants placed to receive no more light than they need add a pleasing accent. The pot of ivy on top receives no light except for the strand that has crept down behind the reflector.

Plate XI. A portable light-garden instead of a lamp can be set on an end table. The colorful flowers and variegated vines climbing from the end zones are interesting and decorative without commanding too much attention in a relaxed living-room environment.

Plate XII. *(Opposite)* The "garden" theme of this breakfast room (shaded from sun by a roofed-in porch) is reinforced by plants growing under portable lights placed in the bottom shelf of a wrought-iron cart. African violets and azaleas receive the light they need, placed under the reflector. A green plant under the bottom glass shelf needs little light and calls attention to the "brick" floor. In the home of Mr. and Mrs. George Anders.

Plate XIII.   A light-garden setup that gives all plants exactly what they need in terms of light rather than decoration. Tall philodendrons are placed on stools behind the fixtures since they do not need more than peripheral light. Low-growing philodendrons and ivy are also given minimal light by placing them on the ends of the table. African violets, mums, and azaleas are placed at the proper distance under the lamps, by elevating the low ones on inverted flower pots.

These are uses of light-gardening that supplement major sources of income. Light-gardening is now only in the beginning stages of commercialization, but those stages are interesting. A greenhouse operator in Ontario grows tomatoes under fluorescent lights affixed beneath his benches, thus utilizing previously wasted space. Growers in California and elsewhere use fluorescents to extend the effectiveness of natural light in their commercial greenhouses, to enable them to have crops ready at exactly the times they want them.

On a smaller scale, we know a woman who supports herself with the weekend sales of her African violets, episcias, and gloxinias, sold from a stand in a large farmer's market. Friday night and all day through 10 P.M. on Saturday, she maintains a stand in the market, from which she dispenses her plants, each with a little mineographed sheet describing its needs. She grows her plants mostly from cuttings in the fluorescent-light-supplemented little greenhouse that her husband built for her to satisfy her hobby interest, long before fluorescent lights were used for plant growth.

FOR PIN MONEY OR MORE

There are many people now who are confronted with the problem of too much leisure for their energies. Early retirement from an active business life may prove boring for the energetic individual who needs more than play to make him happy. Light-gardening for profit can, in such cases, combine the fun of a gardening hobby with the satisfaction of making the hobby at least pay for itself. It it not unknown, either, for a hobby to develop into a full-scale commercial enterprise, and we will give you a few guidelines in that direction presently.

GROWING HERBS TO ORDER

We know a man who grows parsley, dill, chives, marjoram,

Figure 31   Our herb-grower friend uses little peat pots for his herbs,
setting them into a soil-filled window box. Any small pots can be set
into a window box in the same way, for a neatly housed supply of
kitchen herbs.

and rosemary in individual pots to fill the needs of a local
adult-education cooking class. In the first three-session school
year of his experience, he netted almost three hundred dollars for his church. He starts his herbs from seed, grows them
in little peat pots in his light-garden until they are 4-inch
seedlings, and packages them attractively.

Using lightweight polystyrene planter boxes to transport
the seedlings gave him the idea of setting the little pots into
soil in these planters. Thus the window boxes continue to be
of service in the school kitchens, and the seedlings continue
to grow through their peat pots into the potting soil of the
planters.

You can do likewise, if you care to, with many other audiences and markets. Window boxes filled with growing herbs
should be equally salable at church and school fairs, and you
might even find a local grocer who is not bound by the mass-
delivery system of the supermarket. There are so many popular gourmet herbs that you can expand your assortment to fill

the demands of the local market. Just don't forget to label each plant so that you and the customer will know what it is.

Plant-Sitting Service: Housing developments in cities are now so numerous and extensive that many are served by small local newspapers, in which classified ads are inexpensive and productive of results. Such a paper would be the ideal place in which to run a small notice of your willingness to plant-sit for vacationing house-plant owners. Your service would, of course, entail taking the plants into your light-garden, and you should be careful to follow the precautions detailed in chapter 5 on plant quarantine. Your service would be short-lived (and so would your own plants) if you accidentally allowed a diseased plant to infect healthy ones belonging to other customers.

Although we are doing it for friendship's sake, we happen to have several plant visitors in our New York light-garden at the moment. After a flourishing summer outdoors, a fine collection of coleus turned pale and leggy when brought back to our friends' apartment in the city. Furthermore, the painters have been promising to repaint the apartment for several weeks, and plants don't like paint fumes. So we offered refuge in our light-garden, where color came back to the foliage and strength to the stems within a week. We suspect the plants will stay with us until the summer exodus to the country.

This is fun to do for friends, and so little work that a teenager could do it. For strangers, it could be a worthwhile service that would pay its way, too.

Specializing: Growing specialties often comes as a natural outgrowth of your own plant preferences. But it could also be developed in your profit-minded light-garden to meet an established market. There is a constant demand for such plants as African violets, begonias, and geraniums. New varieties in these plants are more popular than the novice might expect.

Seedsmen will sometimes make available trial packages of

annual seeds or test plants, a year before they go onto the general market, so that you can supply the very newest varieties in such limited quantities that they will bring a good price.

Organic gardening: Following the publication of *Silent Spring,* there was deepening concern about plants grown with chemical treatments. Here, too, is a specialty that carries a "price-no-object" tag, if you want to grow vegetable seedlings. Give them their light-garden start, offer them in individual peat pots or market packs, and watch the demand grow as word gets around. Perhaps you can grow ready-to-eat Tiny Tim tomatoes, year-round, if you build a market for them that warrants doing so.

SELLING YOUR KNOWLEDGE

If you like light-gardening well enough to make it a serious hobby, you can become an expert on the subject. Begin keeping accurate records at the outset. Take photographs and slides that illustrate both light-gardening and window-sill gardening effects with similar plants. Build up a file of information and keep it up to date as new developments are reported. You will soon find that, with any gift for self-expression, you can give little talks and write articles on light-gardening. With the tremendous popularity of light-gardening now, there will be no question of finding interested audiences for your stories of what you have done and discovered in your light-garden. Begin with a sample article and a query to the gardening editor of a local paper. Expand to gardening and hobby magazine editors. And contact your power-and-light company to see if they would care to sponsor a series of talks on light-gardening. There's money to be made this way too.

Adult education: A natural result of increased leisure time is an increase in the number and variety of adult-education courses offered by schools, churches, and universities. Once you have established your ability to communicate the knowledge you have, backed with well-researched experience, offer your services as a teacher in light-gardening. It won't pay a great deal, but it may lead to larger income in time.

In something of the same vein, but possibly on a volunteer basis, is the therapy application of light-gardening in hospitals. It is well recognized in medical fields that gardening is both physically and mentally healthful. Light-gardening has the added advantage of being feasible to the patient whose physical disability leaves him with useful hands but limited ability to bend, dig, and exert himself in the outdoor garden. Even from a wheel chair, he can be a gardener.

PROJECTS FOR THE SMALL FRY

Kids love to have a little money of their own to spend, and we of the old-fashioned parental school believe that they should be taught early to earn at least some of it by their own efforts. Too, there are 4-H projects, Scouting projects, and Junior Achievement programs built around gardening. One of our early acquaintances with portable light-gardens came through a planter that was designed specifically for Junior Achievement participants. It consists of a flat equipped with a removable heating pad in the bottom, and a one- or two-tube growth lamp with its reflector, supported above the flat on metal rods. The Juniors use these lamps for growing plants, and their business training has begun when they sell their produce.

Before you set your offspring up with a roadside stand, or help him make his arrangements for the local supermarket to handle all the plants he can produce, better check your local zoning regulations. Junior's business career shouldn't be allowed to run afoul of the law, and in a residential area it may be necessary to obtain a permit before he begins to sell.

GARDEN CLUB IDEAS

Garden clubs are usually interested in raising money. There is nothing more favorable than a light-garden in which you produce out-of-season blooms that will sell profitably. The best project we can think of is to grow ready-to-bloom-soon plants at off seasons. Second-best is to grow specialty plants —each member who has a specialty devoting some of her light-garden space to it—and sell them (again off-season, unless they are very prize plants, in which case they can be sold easily at any time).

Most of the garden-club plant sales are held in spring, and if your light-garden makes it possible for you to have plants ready to bloom a month before they would be expected to do so, you have something salable. To make them most readily salable, they should be well budded. So plant them enough ahead of schedule to have them ready before their season, but keep one that was planted two or three weeks earlier, to show what should be expected.

Garden clubs that gain a reputation for light-grown plants should be able to sell portable light-gardens. People who were delighted with your produce last year will want to do it themselves. So another project is to find out where you can obtain the best price on portable light-gardens that will do the best job under circumstances that prevail in your community. Light-gardening for the garden club that wants to make money from it should be considered at least a two-year project.

LARGE-SCALE PROFITS

If your pin-money projects develop into something that appears to warrant full-scale commercialization, we strongly recommend that you obtain the best business advice available before you invest heavily. The U. S. Chamber of Commerce publishes at least one excellent pamphlet on the principles of starting a successful small business. In addition, you should make a thorough investigation of the horticultural field, including its history as well as its business potential.

This may seem to be unnecessary advice, but we know too

well how easy it is to be carried away by enthusiasm for the new and untried. As a hobby, light-gardening is fascinating and can more than cover its costs. It can even make a profit and still remain at the amateur, avocational level. We believe that it probably has tremendous commercial potential as well, but at this time there is so little commercial application of this very new field that empirical evidence is lacking. The field is open to development. It offers a most interesting challenge. In the next decade, there may be many large-scale success stories of commercial horticulture under artificial light. They just haven't had time to happen yet.

8

A Look into the Future

Throughout this book, we have tried to make a clear distinction between theories that have been thoroughly researched, tested, and proved, and those that are still under experiment. The basic facts about the effect of light on plant growth are no longer a matter for conjecture. That artificial light can be substituted for natural light to produce the same or better plant growth has also been proved. But there is still much to be learned, and experimenting in a relatively new field is always an interesting challenge.

If light-gardening leads you into experimental work, these suggestions may help to focus your attention:

THINGS TO TRY—WITH NEW LIGHTS

1. Find out what infrared light will do if added to the recommended balance of red and blue light. Working with high-voltage incandescents, as suggested in chapter 2, can you speed the bloom of plants without the attendant dangers of regular incandescent lamps?
2. As discussed in chapter 1, plants now appear to respond only to the red and blue wave lengths of light. We are interested in the possibility that plants may have more response to other colors of the spectrum than present theory

indicates. Do plants make use of "trace colors" as they do of trace elements in their food? If they do respond to other colors than red and blue, to what extent and what are their reactions? What colors, if any, are useful trace colors? Experimentation on this question is very easy, because there is a wide variety of colors in fluorescent lamps for visual lighting.

3. Do all plants respond in exactly the same way to the same amounts of colors? We know that some plants appear to bloom best if they are exposed to more red light than other plants require for blooming. Is there a variance in their reactions to blue wave lengths?

4. Does a twisted fluorescent tube (described in chapter 2) do anything for plants that is a substantial improvement over straight tubes?

THINGS TO TRY—WITH TIMING

1. Commercial growers use artificial light now primarily for speeding the bloom of long-day plants and delaying the bloom of short-day plants. How many interruptions in a single dark period will result in the plant reacting as though a new day had started? How short can these interruptions be in long-day plants? How short in short-day plants?

2. Can artificial light be used to shorten a plant's requirements for rest between growth periods?

3. How long can you actually leave a light-garden alone if it is fully automated with sprinklers, humidifiers, and timed day-and-night periods?

THINGS TO TRY—WITH FOOD AND WATER

1. In a mixed light-garden with flowers of varying requirements for moisture and feeding, how much can be done with automatic timers?

2. Do light-garden plants react any differently to slow-release fertilizers than outdoor plants do? Does the everyday light of a light-garden stimulate plants to such an extent that they use up a year's supply of slow-release plant food in less than a year?

THINGS TO TRY—WITH PROPAGATION AND GROWTH

1. Do growth-control chemicals react any differently on plants grown in a light-garden than on outdoor plants? Are they as effective in stunting the growth of long-stemmed plants when the plants are grown under the extra stimulation of light every day? Do all plants react in the same way to dwarfing chemicals?
2. Can all biennials be made to bloom twice a year under lights?
3. Will light-garden growth extend the productive life of plants that live and bloom outdoors for only a few years? Or will the extra stimulation of light shorten their lives?
4. Can seeds—any or all—be germinated in the light? If not all, which seeds will germinate without darkness?

THINGS TO TRY—WITH NEW MATERIALS

1. Can black plastic be used in the light-garden as it is outdoors for mulching? Can it be used for shading short-day plants?
2. Keep an open mind to the light-garden applications of anything and everything as it is offered to the horticultural market.

THINGS TO TRY—IN UNTRIED PLACES

1. Can artificial lights be used to extend bloom in the outdoor garden?

2. Can a light-garden be built effectively into an outdoor area or a gazebo?

3. Will light-gardening have any important application to travel into outer space and other planets? We know that plants are now being grown on submarines; under the ice in an antarctic encampment; and in a man's home in Texas, fifty feet underground. Can a light-garden supply food to sustain life in a bomb shelter?

PART II

Compatible
Light-Garden Plants

There are no seasons in light-gardening except those caused by rest periods that some plants require. Plants that need rest periods can either be taken out of the light-garden and put into a dark place without watering or left in a peripheral area, such as a corner on the floor. In this list, we have indicated plants that need rest, and when they should be rested.

Any purchased plant intended for the outdoor garden will benefit from a month under lights, if it is acquired before the ground is ready. Nursery-grown plants especially are often sold when they are in bloom. They should be allowed to finish blooming under lights before they are transplanted.

In this plant list, the times recommended for setting out plants, their blooming, and their germinating times, all relate to plants that are grown out of doors in the general vicinity of New York City. Many seed packets show this as Zone 3 on their maps; it is listed as Zone 7 on the U. S. Department of Agriculture map.

Some plants will eventually change their growth cycles if grown entirely under lights, but it may take three or four growth cycles to complete the change and establish new habits.

When you grow from seed, no matter when you plant them, the growth cycle to blooming time under lights will not be longer, but may be shorter than outdoors.

If your light-garden is relatively idle during the summer months, it's best not to start any new plants after April first until you return to concentrated indoor gardening. Casual attention will maintain most of your light-garden plants that are well established by summertime; or you may prefer to do as the Johnstons do—take all the plants to the outdoor garden and reserve the light-garden for other seasons.

Distances below the light source recommended in this section apply to the average two-channel light-garden of the average light-gardening hobbyist. They do not always agree exactly with distances used by scientific experimenters, but reflect the successful experience of serious amateurs. Truly scientific experiments conducted by universities and other researchers have been done in light chambers where overhead lights cover the entire ceiling, packed as closely together as is mechanically possible. Hobbyists would not care to foot the light bill nor the construction cost of such laboratory equipment.

RECOMMENDED TEMPERATURES

Temperatures considered ideal for developing potted plants, seedlings, and seeds vary considerably with species. Presently available statistics all are based on greenhouse gardening, whereas light-gardening is more closely related to window-sill gardening. Even within the realm of greenhouse gardening, there is a wide range of temperature recommendations for the same plants. Commercial greenhouse operations are usually aimed at keeping the operating costs down and setting flower buds as early as possible. Scientific experiments are geared to creating ideal conditions, often on a tight budget, and always under laboratory controls. Light-gardening is a hobby with which to live comfortably. So the temperatures we recommend may vary considerably from those considered ideal; nevertheless, our recommendations are reliable.

If you plan to devote your light-gardening efforts largely

to one type of plant, you can choose a location that best provides that plant's preferred greenhouse temperature—the
coolest part of the house for plants that do best in a cool
greenhouse, for example. But if you want to grow a variety of
plants and make your light-garden an integral part of your
living arrangements as we do, the plants must adapt themselves to temperatures that you find comfortable. As we have
said, plants are surprisingly adaptable. We have found that
the majority of plants are quite tolerant of temperatures in the
70° F. range. With an ideal temperature, your plants may set
more buds and flower more profusely than they would in temperatures that are higher or lower, but they *will* bloom in
your comfortable living room.

Early in light-gardening experience, the Johnston team de-
voted an unheated room to this hobby. But it was not a place
in which to live, and much greater enjoyment came from
locating the light-garden where it could be seen and shared
with friends. If you too wish to share your winter gardening
pleasure, keep in mind that light-gardening is an improvement on window-sill gardening, and can be an extension of
greenhouse gardening, in which you can mix and match your
plants at will, taking the small risk that some of them will not
do as well as they might in a greenhouse. If you want to specialize in one plant, chances are that your light-garden will
serve as a source of supply for a few specimen plants to be
put on display in your living room, and you can cater to that
plant's temperature needs without necessarily living in the
light-garden yourself.

There are many more plants than we have included here
that can be grown successfully in your light-garden. By com-
paring unlisted plants with similar plants that we have included, you can judge how to treat them.

Plants for Maximum Light

Seedlings: place 4 to 6 inches below lights.
Mature plants: place 6 to 10 inches below lights.

Abronia umbellata (Sand Verbena; Wild Lantana), peren., 5 to 8 inches

An excellent plant for permanent light-garden use, especially in hanging baskets. Remove seed husks and sow ¼-inch deep in vermiculite. Start some in January, and follow with successive plantings two or three weeks apart, to extend blooming period. Seeds normally germinate in twenty days. Started in January, should bloom in June of first year. When sprouts show, transplant into sandy loam, keeping fairly dry, and place under lights. For outdoor garden, set out when soil is thoroughly warm. Stem cuttings or division, taken just before or just after bloom, will increase your collection.

Althea rosea (Hollyhock) annual; bien.; peren., 5 to 9 feet

We prefer the perennials, which we start from seed in December or January. Sown ½-inch deep in vermiculite, seed normally germinates in ten days. When sprouted, transplant into peat pots filled with any ordinary garden soil. They have a long tap root and do not re-establish readily, so potting in peat pots makes it easier to set them out when frost is gone. When 9 inches tall, pinch back to 6 inches. Given a head start in the light-garden, they may bloom earlier than their normal July and August schedule. They readily self-sow, but if yours revert to single blooms after a few years, dig them out and start with fresh seeds. Seeds sown in July and put under lights when sprouted can be set out in October for bloom the next year. Annuals should be started in January. Naturally, hollyhocks are too tall for light-gardens, but very popular for screening in the outdoor garden. Easy to grow, they need watering during dry spells.

Alyssum saxatile compactum (Basket-of-Gold; Gold Dust; Madwort) hardy peren., 6 to 8 inches

Our own Basket-of-Gold came as a gift from a neighbor, who was dividing hers in midsummer when they had bloomed and spread to the point of encroaching on other flowers in her garden border. They have self-sown, spread, and continued to be increasingly attractive plants in the three years we have had them bordering our lily bed in Connecticut. Yet they are said by some growers to be difficult to move when mature, and therefore starting from seed is recommended. Sow ¼-inch deep in vermiculite. When sprouts are large enough to handle, they can be potted in half vermiculite and half peat moss, preferably in peat pots. Seeds germinate rapidly any time, flower in six to eight weeks, bloom freely. Started in August, permanently potted for light-garden residence so that they won't spread, they will bloom from December throughout the winter months in the light-garden. After several months of rest, they will bloom again. We like our light-gardens to resemble an outdoor garden as much as possible, and for that reason, we value these low-growing border plants, which make an attractive underlining of grey-green foliage when they are not in bloom.

Anemone Pulsatilla (Pasque-Flower) peren., 7 to 12 inches

Best started from purchased plants, root or stem cuttings, or by division, this little rock-garden favorite gets off to a slow start, blooming in about six months from seed. The little plant is available at garden centers in the fall. It can be set outdoors in October for bloom the following spring or placed immediately in the light-garden for bloom in the winter. If it is slow to bloom, raise it closer to the light source. Likes sandy loam with a little peat moss added, and fertilizing will increase its bloom. Once its gets into production it's an interesting addition to the light-garden family, since its blooms are followed by long, feathery plumes that continue the show. If you start from seed, which germinates normally in about fifteen days, transplant the seedlings to peat pots for eventual outdoor residence, as it resists moving.

Antirrhinum hybrids (Snapdragon) hardy annual, 12 to 20 inches

Seed germinates in ten days without bottom heat, sooner if heated. The very fine seed needs to be barely covered by vermiculite. When seedlings are two inches tall, transplant to peat pots if they are to go outdoors or to permanent containers for light-garden residence. We prefer the dwarf types indoors (don't need stakes) but start the taller varieties late in February or early March to be put outdoors in frost-free soil that is at least moderately rich. We always keep a reserve on hand in the light-garden in case we need to replace plants that were nipped by a late frost. Seeds started in July for light-garden plants should produce flowers by Christmas. Indoors they like moderate to cool temperatures, and a light growing medium; half vermiculite and half peat moss is recommended. Staggered plantings will provide continuous bloom, if you sow seeds at about three-month intervals. If you remove the side shoots, one single spike will bloom and will probably need support. We often pot several in a 5-inch pot and allow them to branch naturally. If flowers are sparse, the light-garden may be too warm. This is a long-day plant, but seedlings do well on a short-day schedule.

Arabis albida (Wall Cress) hardy peren., 8 to 12 inches

This easy-to-grow plant can be propagated by division, by

root cuttings, or from seed, which germinates in five days and self-sows if given the opportunity. It likes sandy, well-drained soil, and for permanent indoor living, it can grow happily in vermiculite alone if it is fertilized at regular intervals. Seed started in September or October and set in the light-garden when sprouts show will be ready to bloom outdoors in the rock garden as soon as frost is gone. They can be divided and some brought back after bloom to do a repeat performance in the light-garden during the autumn. As permanent light-garden plants, they are likely to bloom twice a year according to their outdoor cycle of spring and fall.

Arctotis stoechadifolia (African Daisy) annual, 12 inches (dwarf); 30 to 48 inches

Seeds sown in January will produce plants ready to set out when soil is frost-free, to bloom in the light-garden by the end of April or the middle of May. The dwarf variety is the natural choice for the light-garden, and makes a good plant for the winter light-garden. It is easy to grow in any ordinary soil, a bit on the sandy, poor side, and it doesn't mind either heat or drought, so don't overwater it.

Argemone grandiflora (Prickly Poppy) hardy annual, 2 to 3 feet

This showy plant grows too tall for the average light-garden, but is a delight in the outdoor garden. We plant seeds in April, sowing them ¼-inch deep in vermiculite for easy transplanting of the seedlings into peat pots. The seeds germinate in fifteen days, sooner with bottom heat. We set out some as soon as the ground is warm, holding a reserve against possible frost, and thus have them in bloom earlier than their July and August schedule. They like to be kept warm and dry in well-drained sandy loam. Spectacular for a color accent in the outdoor garden, they are also excellent cutting flowers.

Armeria maritima (Thrift) hardy peren., 8 to 12 inches

Seeds sown about the first of March normally germinate in ten days and if seedlings are set in the light-garden for a month or so, they should bloom during the first year in June or July. Under lights, they will bloom again in the winter, and if you want to import some from your outdoor garden, simply divide their roots after bloom, pot them in light, sandy soil, and don't overwater. A delightful accent in the light-garden because they are evergreen, they are also valued as one of the best of the everlastings, excellent for your dried-flower arrangements.

Asclepias tuberosa (Butterfly-Weed; Pleurisy Root; Orange Milkweed) hardy peren., 12 to 20 inches

One of our personal favorites in Connecticut, because it is not only colorful and graceful in our outdoor garden when it blooms in midsummer, but is constantly alive with butter-flies. When the blooms are gone, the seed pods are interesting, useful in dried arrangements, and fun to use in starting new plants. Seeds are slow to germinate usually, so we give them bottom heat to have sprouts in about two weeks. We plant them ¼-inch deep in vermiculite in January or February. Then we transplant the seedlings into individual peat pots, keep them in the light-garden until they are tall enough to attract notice, because we treat them as the wildflowers they are, and plant them on a warm, sloping site where, unless visible or marked, they may be stepped on. The roots are brittle, and hence difficult to move, so although we could divide them in the fall, prune them back, and put them into the light-garden, we prefer to pick a pod or two, let it dry for a month, and start the seeds for a new batch. If you should happen to see some in bloom when visiting a friend, as we did, but be un-able to be on hand when the seed pods are ready for picking, you can purchase a plant or two from a wildflower dealer.

Aster hybrids (Michaelmas daisy; Perennial aster) hardy peren., 12 to 24 inches

Sometimes treated as a half-hardy annual, they are best propagated from seed, which normally germinates in fifteen days. Sow seeds $^1/_{16}$-inch deep in vermiculite in March if they are to go outdoors, or four to five months before you expect bloom, if they are to stay in the light-garden. When seedlings appear, transplant them into peat pots with a little vermiculite in the bottom of each pot to provide drainage. Keep them carefully watered, and leave them under the lights until the ground is really warm in the outdoor garden. Then set them into rich soil and they'll bloom from late summer until frost. Asters are short-day plants, and if you are keeping them in the light-garden watch them closely for signs of budding. As soon as buds begin to show color, give them only ten hours of light, and move them into the darkness for the other fourteen hours each day. This long-night treatment will speed them into faster bloom, producing longer stems. Short-night treatment means shorter stems; slower flowering. Asters need well-enriched soil, indoors or out. Manure is recommended, and can be provided even indoors by feeding them with the prepared dehydrated kind. Fish-emulsion fertilizers also work well on them.

Borago officinalis (Borage) annual, 12 to 20 inches

Like most of the plants in your herb garden, this one is usually started from seed. Sow about ¼-inch deep around the first of March in vermiculite, so that the seedlings can easily be transplanted into peat pots. This is one of the many plants that resents transplanting, and if you plan to grow your herbs all year round indoors, transplant the seedlings into the permanent herb garden as soon as they can be handled easily. It can go outdoors when the soil is warm, to bloom all summer with lovely blue flowers that attract bees. Despite the fact that this plant resists transplanting when it is young, once established, it can be divided after bloom. So if a friend offers you some from her outdoor herb garden, accept it gratefully and just be careful not to break the roots when you take your share to plant indoors. It has no particular preference as to soil, and its foliage is delightfully aromatic. It's the foliage rather than the blooms that you use in salads.

Browallia speciosa (Browallia) half-hardy annual, 12 to 18 inches

Although it may be six months after you plant the seeds that this plant comes into bloom, once it begins blossoming it remains almost constantly in production. But like most plants that bloom "continuously", the flowers will be prettier if it is given a rest once in a while, and to insure literally constant bloom, staggered plantings are recommended. Seeds germinate normally in fifteen days. If you started in January, expect bloom in midsummer; in July, midwinter bloom. Especially attractive in hanging baskets. This plant is also good if planted in quantity in a flat or bulb pan. Highly recommended for light-garden purposes, but it can also do well in the outdoor garden if you wait until the soil is thoroughly warm before you set it out. It likes a mixture of ¾ loam and ¼ sand, and is otherwise undemanding. Extra hours of light do not affect growth. Nip off bushy growth during its early stages, and you'll have better bloom and shape when it matures. If you set it outdoors in summer, leave it in pots and bring it back into the light-garden for winter.

Cacti

Desert plants are accustomed to cool nights and a merciless sun beating down on them during the daytime. The plants that survive are those that carry their own store of water within their cells, use it sparingly, and wait like camels for the next chance to drink. So the one thing the cactus grower must remember is not to overwater the plants.

Contrary to expectation, some cacti prefer not to be in direct sun, and do best when kept on the edge of the light-garden shelf, but close (4 to 6 inches) below the tubes. They want an alkaline soil, very sandy and porous, and can easily be propagated by stem cuttings. When you take a stem cutting, however, rub powdered charcoal over the cut end of the stem before rooting it, and also over the wound until it stops bleeding.

In the Carrière light-garden we started cactus from seed. The seed is very fine, and very slow to germinate. We mixed it with sand, scattered it on the surface of a bed of sand with charcoal under it, and misted the surface. A few weeks later we began to see results—tiny sprouts that often resembled grains of sand themselves, sometimes grey, sometimes green, sometimes even brown, began to appear. So we gently pulled them out of their bed, leaving others to sprout later, as they did over a period of six months, and transplanted them. Each tiny cactus went into a little plastic coffee scoop with drainage holes provided by heating a toasting fork and immediately punching holes through the plastic, so as not to break it. A lump of charcoal went into each little container, followed by a mixture of sand and bird gravel, and the little cactus was on its slow way to growth and eventual maturity, which in some cases would be years. We set up our cactus garden of gay-colored scoops on a tray filled with sand, and put it close under the fluorescent tubes to grow.

Unfortunately, our story of growing cactus from seed was a short one. The kittens found the back way into the light-garden, mistook the sand for kitty litter, and dutifully scratched until every miniscule plant was lost.

Calendula officinalis (Pot Marigold) annual, 12 to 20 inches

This is a popular house plant as well as an addition to the

outdoor garden, since it normally blooms for a long period, from early summer until frost. Best germinated from seed sown $^1/_{16}$-inch deep in vermiculite in March, transplanted when sprouted to a mixture of ¾ loam and ¼ sand, kept on the dry side. It can be set into the outdoor garden when soil is warm. As a light-garden plant, it prefers to be kept fairly cool during the winter. Planted in July, it will be ready for its permanent pot in September. Planted in December, you can pot it permanently in February. Kept dry, it will then bloom the following November or May, respectively. For best-of-show in specimen flowers, pinch off all but one terminal bud. For fun in light-gardening, watch its petals close when you turn off the lights.

Calliopsis (see *Coreopsis*)

Callistephus (see *Aster* hybrids)

Calonyction aculeatum (Moonflower) half-hardy peren., 8 to 20 feet

Seed germinates in 5 days, but must be soaked overnight before starting in March or April with bottom heat in vermiculite. Since the seeds are so large, we start ours by planting three in a little peat pot, which must be filled with ½ loam, ½ sand and not fertilized until the seedlings are 2 inches high; or with vermiculite, fertilized as soon as the sprouts show. Too much fertilizer will produce profuse foliage but few flowers throughout the life of the plant, yet it likes to be set out into rich soil. When it's young, it's fun in the light-garden, because we enjoy watching the slender little vine of stem crinkle like a corkscrew until it finds something to latch onto. Inevitably, we feel sympathetic toward its efforts, and give it a bit of string. It thanks us by winding itself around the string and climbing against the walls of the light-garden, where it can stay if the light-garden is large enough, because it can

climb up one wall, across the top, and down again. It blooms
only at night, when the lights are turned off, so its companion
flower, the Morning Glory, is more fun if you are home all
day. But certainly a Moonflower is a conversation piece for
the light-gardener who is home only in the evening, and it
stays open until noon the next day outdoors. If your entire
light-garden is geared for only ten hours of light, this short-
day plant is a good choice. This is an interesting plant in the
outdoor garden especially. Its pale blooms are delightful in
moonlight, or lighted by distant garden lights. But in the
Johnston outdoor garden, with its seaside atmosphere and
light, the moonflower behaves almost like a long-day plant,
which contradicts its habit of blooming only after sunset. At
any rate, it does best if started in the light-garden, and blooms
four or five weeks earlier than neighboring plants that were
not treated as we have described.

Campanula medium (Canterbury Bells) hardy annual, 6 to 12
inches

This is an especially attractive plant if you exhibit it under
plant-growth fluorescents, which intensify its blue color.
There are not too many blue flowers that can be seen to advantage indoors, because natural-colored artificial light tends
to fade out blue flowers. Seed germinates in twenty days, but
could do it in ten if you give it bottom heat. Sown in January,
it acts as a biennial through the second year, then dies. To
continue its blooms, which occur six months after planting
seeds as a rule, you can either divide the plant just before or
just after bloom, or you can take stem cuttings. New plants
will start from either. This is a pretty plant in the year-round
light-garden, and it can be set outdoors when the soil is warm,
to bloom in early summer when you need color. It wants rich,
well-drained soil, and should be kept pruned for bushy
growth and prolific flowers. At summer's end, pot some for
the light-garden.

Carnation (see *Dianthus*)

Celosia cristata (Cockscomb) half-hardy annual, 9 to 12 inches (dwarf); 12 to 30 inches

Sow seeds in January, and they will germinate normally in ten days. They will then be ready to set outdoors when ground is frost-free, and will be large enough to bloom in early June after having lived in the light-garden since their sprouts showed. *Never* prune them. They want their average garden loam to be kept fairly moist, and when they have bloomed and are at their prime, they can be cut and dried for dried-flower arrangements. It will improve the bloom if you enrich the soil with fish-emulsion or commercially prepared manure while they are outdoors. They may be inclined to spread widely, so allow plenty of room in the light-garden if you grow the dwarf types there. This is a short-day plant but vegetative growth is stimulated and flowers delayed if grown on long-day schedule.

Centaurea Cineraria (Dusty Miller) half-hardy peren., 12 to 18 inches

Since the seed may normally take longer than its expected ten days to germinate, this is one to which we always give bottom heat when planting the seeds. Once the seedlings have come up, they may still be reluctant to mature, taking up to eight months before they come into bloom. If it's bloom you want (most people value this plant for its lovely grey-green foliage), it's best to buy the plants, or to start them from stem cuttings or division. We pinch off the bloom, which is relatively insignificant, so that the foliage will have added strength, because we love the cool, feathery look of any of the grey-green foliages, indoors or out. Seed started in July or August should produce seedlings that can be set out in your rock garden next spring. Started in January, they can go out in the fall. Although this is not a reliably hardy plant north of New York City, because it can't stand cold wet feet in winter, it may self-sow, so all is not lost if you set it outdoors even in our northern climate. In the permanent light-garden, it is one of our favorites—not for bloom, but for foliage.

Centaurea cyanus (Bachelors-Button; Bluebottle; Cornflower; Ragged Robin; Ragged Sailor) hardy annual, 12 to 18 inches

Again that valued touch of blue is available, this time in something that you can pick off and tuck into a gentleman's buttonhole. Outdoors, it blooms from July until frost, provided that you set it out when the ground is warm, from seeds that you sowed in February. Seeds normally germinate in ten days, but since they may take longer, it's best to give them bottom heat. Outdoors, it often self-sows, but indoors or out, it will grow better bloom on stronger stems if you pinch it back. We have found that seeds sown in February, with seedlings put under lights when sprouted, can be brought to bloom in April in the light-garden.

Chrysanthemum peren., 12 to 30 inches

PROPAGATION BY CUTTINGS: As winter approaches we take stem cuttings, dip them into a rooting powder and plant about a dozen to a market pack holding vermiculite (or any similar medium). The market pack goes under lights at any convenient spot until roots develop. Then we repot three into each 5-inch pot holding a standard soil mixture. Now this is important: the potted plants are set about 8 inches below the light, centered or slightly off center. Give them fourteen hours of light. After three weeks pinch them back once. Leave them under light for another three to four months, improving shape by pruning as necessary. Now start them on a ten-hour light schedule. When the first flower buds appear:

If you want a few big flowers, pinch off all side buds and allow top terminal bud on each to develop.

If you want many small flowers allow all buds to develop.

To retard bloom just leave plants on long-day light. They like a rather cool environment but will tolerate up to 68° F. for bud setting.

DWARFING: Chrysanthemums are the major plants on which dwarfing compounds have been thoroughly tested. Follow the directions on the package of Phosphon, which was the first of the dwarfing chemicals to be authorized by the U. S. Dept. of Agriculture for ornamental plants. The newer chemicals intended to do the same job are still under test, and will perhaps prove equally effective. By following the instructions exactly, you can raise chrysanthemums to whatever precise height you wish. As we have mentioned earlier, these new dwarfing compounds do not reduce the size of the blossoms, but make the stems shorter between nodes, the leaves greener in appearance, and the plant in general, more compact.

Chrysanthemum coccineum (Painted Daisy; Pyrethrum) peren., 1 to 2 feet

Chrysanthemum maximum (Shasta Daisy) hardy peren., 15 to 30 inches

With bottom heat, seeds of both should germinate in four or five days. Start in January, and when seedlings are large enough to handle, set them into the light-garden to grow sturdy stems and leaves before setting out in spring when the soil is frost-free. The dwarf varieties (and you can create your own by using dwarfing chemicals) are happy in the year-round light-garden. Outdoors, we mulched ours in the New Jersey garden with cocoa-bean hulls and peat moss. The cocoa-bean hulls are full of nitrogen, which made the leaves greener and bushier and the stems longer—so long, in fact, that a six-foot girl who was visiting us said, "This is the first time a daisy ever looked me in the eye." Cutting the blooms prolongs blooming life.

Dianthus barbatus (Sweet William) half-hardy bien., 6 to 12 inches.

Dianthus Caryophyllus (hardy Carnation) annual, 12 to 18 inches

Dianthus chinensis (China Pink) annual, 12 to 18 inches

Dianthus deltoides (Maiden Pink; Spink) peren., 4 to 9 inches

Dianthus plumarius (Grass Pink; Scotch Pink) peren., 12 to 15 inches

Seeds in this family will all germinate normally in five days, and are easy to start in vermiculite. Sweet William is one of our outdoor-garden favorites, where it readily self-sows, and each year we divide some of the plants in the fall, pot them in ordinary soil treated with dwarfing compound (because the variety we have doesn't happen to be naturally dwarf), and bring them into the light-garden. Sweet William seldom blooms the first year, but if you start the seed in December and put the seedlings under lights, you should have blooms the following midsummer, having set the plants out when the soil was warm. They like good air circulation around them, and prefer a cool location. The Wee Willie natural dwarf is a delight in the light-garden, because it grows only four to six inches tall. We leave most of our plants out in the garden over the winter, mulched with leaves. The old ones that have bloomed die off, but the suckers that have grown from them take their place.

The hardy Carnation, similar to the florist's carnation but a little smaller bloom, can be propagated from seeds sown about the first of April, put under lights until the soil is warm, and then set out to bloom from August until frost. You can also take cuttings of the permanent light-garden residents in the winter, any time from December to March, root them, put them under lights until their buds show color, and then treat them as long-day plants with at least fourteen hours, preferably 16 hours, of light. Take off all buds except one to make a better bloom on each plant. Not hardy in cold country outdoors, they may be treated as biennial or perennial in the South, and are always a light-garden attraction. By staggering the planting or rooting of cuttings, you can have light-garden carnations in bloom all the time.

The little low-growing pinks are delightful in the light-garden, because even when they are not in bloom, their foliage is pretty. We keep them potted so that they won't follow their normal inclination to spread all over the map. They can be started from seed and expected to bloom in about ten weeks; or you can divide them and simply plant the divisions, which will continue to increase and make new plants. Seeds sown in January will bloom a second time before the next January, and bloom continues well especially if you pick off the old blossoms.

Dimorphotheca aurantiaca (Cape Marigold; Cape Daisy; Star of the Veldt; African Daisy) half-hardy annual, 12 to 18 inches

Sow the seeds in vermiculite, and if you give them bottom heat, they will probably germinate in five days. We like to start some in January, and stagger the plantings in order to extend the blooming period. Those started in January should bloom in the light-garden in April, and you can keep them blooming indoors or out until fall, by staggering them about three weeks apart. They prefer sandy loam, and should not be set outdoors until the soil is thoroughly warm. In the light-garden, keep them close to the light and water them sparingly, pruning them for bushier, shorter growth.

Eschscholtzia californica (California Poppy) hardy annual, 8 to 20 inches

The poppy family responds well to lights, and we have found that a combination of cool white and warm white fluorescents increases the bloom as compared to those kept under plant-growth lamps. Nevertheless, if you keep them close enough to the plant-growth lamps, they will bloom. Sow the seeds on top of a tray filled with vermiculite, cover very lightly, and water them in. With bottom heat, they should germinate in about five days. When the sprouts are large enough to handle, transplant into peat pots filled with sandy soil if they are to be set outdoors, as they dislike transplanting. If you are going to keep them in the light-garden, pot them in permanent pots that are small enough to keep them under control when they are mature, as they have a tendency to spread. Sown in March, they should bloom by midsummer; and sown in the fall, you may expect winter bloom in the light-garden.

Felicia amelloides (Blue Daisy) hardy annual or half-hardy peren., 1 to 2½ feet

Similar in culture to the Shasta Daisy, we grow this plant from seed sown in February. It normally germinates in fifteen days, and is ready to set out after frost is gone, to bloom by early June. It transplants easily from the sandy loam with good drainage that is its preference, and has a long blooming period. We have experimented with bringing it indoors to the light-garden when it stops blooming, and sometimes it will bloom again after about eight weeks of resting under lights. Its indoor cycle has not, apparently, become firmly established, so it's fun to see what each plant will do when it's time for the second blooming.

Gaillardia aristata (Blanket-Flower; Perennial Gaillardia) hardy peren., 18 to 30 inches

Gaillardia pulchella (Annual Blanket-Flower; Gay Flower)
hardy annual, 12 to 20 inches

Because these plants take up quite a bit of room, we don't
usually keep them in the permanent light-garden. But we
have found that the light-garden acts like a cold frame in
getting them started, and that they will bloom a month earlier
after their light-garden beginning. With bottom heat, you can
expect the seed to germinate in about ten days, and we sow
them in December to have them in bloom the following July.
They can also be propagated by division or by root or stem
cuttings in the fall or early spring, to be given their light-
garden start and set outdoors the following spring or fall.
While they are in the light-garden, we keep them cut back
to conserve space, and this increases their initial sturdiness.
Gaillardia are durable, attractive plants, that stand drought
and hot weather without complaint.

Geranium (see *Pelargonium*)

Gerbera jamesoni (African Daisy; Barberton Daisy; Trans-
vaal Daisy) half-hardy peren., 12 to 24 inches

Given bottom heat, seeds should germinate in about fifteen
days, but be patient, as they might take a bit longer. We like
to stagger the plantings for extended bloom, and keep some
permanently in the light-garden. Sow the first seeds in February and continue sowing through May. Plant the seeds
individually in vermiculite-filled peat pots, placing each seed
in an upright position and leaving the top uncovered. Water
carefully—they need perfect drainage, and don't forget the
plastic covering to help them germinate. They are difficult
to grow outdoors in the North, because they are very sensitive
to frost. So be certain not to set them out until the weather
is really warm. Dig them into rich loam, a little sandy, if they
go outdoors. And if you keep them permanently in the light-

garden, set the peat pots into pots of loam for their permanent growth. Place them at the back of the light-garden because they are tall when mature, and don't expect them to bloom in much less than a year from the time you sow the seed. They're difficult, but challenging.

Gypsophila elegans grandiflora (Baby's-Breath) hardy annual, 10 to 18 inches

Usually grown from seed, which germinates normally in three or four months, this one also can be propagated from root or stem cuttings, or by dividing when it has finished blooming. For continuous bloom, sow the seed in staggered lots two weeks apart, allowing four months until bloom. If you have this delightful edging plant in your outdoor garden, divide the plants in September or October, put them into pots that you can bring into the light-garden and plant tight enough so that it can't spread, and you'll have bloom from December through the winter under lights. This is another of our favorites in the dainty category, and is excellent for use in dried flower arrangements. It likes ordinary soil without acidity.

Helianthus annuus (Sunflower) half-hardy annual, 8 to 12 feet

Obviously too tall for permanent light-garden residence, this is nevertheless one of the flowers that we start in our light-gardens because doing so gives us an extra month or even two months of spectacular bloom. The seeds germinate in five days normally, and we sow them individually, three to a peat pot, in vermiculite. When they have sprouted, they go into the light-garden until late April or early May, keeping several plants on reserve in the light-garden until the first of June, just in case of a late frost. They attract both birds and people. For the former, their seeds are sufficient to suggest building nests near the source of supply, and we seldom find enough at the end of the season that can be collected and saved for next year's planting. For the latter, we have known people to make special trips from miles around just to see the Johnston sunflowers blooming in June, when nobody expects them until August. They are not particular as to soil, but of course their height indicates staking if they are set out in a wind-swept place, even though their stems are exceedingly sturdy. We have ours near a tall fence.

Helichrysum bracteatum (Strawflower) hardy annual, 12 to 30 inches

An easy plant for beginners, and rewarding even after bloom because they are valued for their drying qualities, strawflowers are a delight in the light-garden. Seeds germinate in five days under normal circumstances, and will bloom in about three months or four months from sowing time. They like to be kept warm, and prefer light soil mixtures. If you set them out, wait until the leaves on your trees have begun to look like leaves instead of buds. Don't try to keep the tall ones in your light-garden. They are not rewarding enough.

Hibiscus palustris (Rose Mallow) peren., 3 to 6 feet

This plant is excellent for the Johnston garden, because it is tolerant of the salt-spray atmosphere of the seaside, and prefers sandy soil. Since seeds are sometimes slow to germinate, it's well to give them bottom heat so that you'll be certain to have sprouts in a couple of weeks. It can also be propagated by division either just before or just after bloom. Despite its height, we keep it in our winter light-garden, setting it close to the lights and turning it frequently to balance its shapely growth. Started under lights in December when the sprouts show, you can have it in bloom in the first midsummer season. If you divide plants in the outdoor garden in late spring, give them a light-garden boost until September or October, and then set them out for bloom the following year. If you

start from seeds in midwinter, set the plants out when the
ground is free of all frost.

Iberis umbellata (Candytuft) hardy annual or hardy peren.,
8 to 15 inches

Another of the dainty, long-blooming plants that makes a
charming accent in the light-garden. Given bottom heat, the
seeds should germinate in about ten days, and if you want
bloom all winter, stagger the sowing—some in June, some in
July, and the rest in August. Or divide the clumps in late
fall, pot them up and put them in the light-garden, for midwinter bloom that will continue to early spring. You can set
them outdoors when frost is gone, and they will bloom from
early spring through summer. They may be a bit weak the
first year, but a light-garden start will produce better blooms
and sturdier plants. They do best under a combination of
warm white and cool white fluorescents in the light-garden,
and like their soil quite light and well-drained. For permanent light-garden residence, they will grow well in soil to
which perlite is added, if the soil tends to hold too much
moisture.

Ipomoea purpurea (Morning-Glory) half-hardy annual, 6 to
15 feet

Like its relative, the Moonflower, the Morning-Glory is a
conversation piece in the light-garden, but practicable only
if your light-garden is large enough to accommodate it. It
can be trained to climb up one side, across the top, and down
the other side, and since it is one of our favorites outdoors,
we are willing to work with it in order to enjoy it longer.
Soak the seeds overnight, then plant three to a small peat-
potful of vermiculite in March. Once they have sprouted,
which shouldn't take more than five days, put them under
the lights keeping them close to the tubes, and not allowing
them to dry out. In about two months (if you start the first

batch in March), they should be sturdy enough to set outdoors. It's a good idea to stagger the seed planting, which is easy because they are such large seeds, so that you won't lose any in a late frost, as has happened in our Connecticut garden. Once they start blooming, which should be in early or midsummer, they will continue until frost. We have found that by planting them on our westward-facing terrace, we have them blooming from late morning throughout the afternoon, because the sun doesn't reach them until about noon, and from then on, in the long summer days, they receive full light until close to sunset. With a southern or eastern exposure, they will bloom earlier in the day, and be finished sooner. For a cramped light-garden area, you can nip the plants back to the height that you can accommodate, and they will produce more blooms on less vine. But we are always fascinated to watch the rapidity with which the vine curls around a string hung to guide it upward, and are quite satisfied with the way nature grows these plants. Morning-Glories will bloom earlier in a warm temperature—70 to 75° F.

Lantana Camara (Lantana; Red or Yellow Sage; Surinam Tea Plant), 18 to 30 inches; 3 to 5 feet

There are several successful methods of propagating Lantana. They are not always easy from seed, sown in early March with bottom heat to bloom by July, because they sometimes germinate very slowly. They can be started from cuttings taken in the fall, and kept at 60 to 65° F. temperature until rooted. If they are going outdoors into the garden, it will be sound procedure to set them out in pots that can be dug up easily and brought back indoors before frost. Ever-blooming and fun to play with, we have found that they make excellent pot plants, and are lovely in baskets or lavabos in the trailing variety. They bloom best for us under a 40-watt Power-Twist combined with a 40-watt plant-growth fluorescent.

Lavandula spica (Lavender; French Lavender) hardy peren.,
1 to 2 feet

Because a garden is attractive to the nose as well as to the
eye, we always like to have something that gives off a pleasant scent without being overpowering. Too much lavender
is *too* much indoors, but you can settle for one or two plants,
or grow it outdoors in the open garden—or both, of course.
Easiest propagation is from stem or root cuttings, but there's
nothing hard about starting the seeds. They germinate in
about 15 days normally, and can be sown any time if you
want lavender as a permanent resident in your light-garden.
The foliage is as interesting as the flowers, and it's the foliage that provides the scent. Seeds started in January should
blossom within six months. Don't fertilize the plants if you
want the scent, as fertilizer tends to dull the fragrance. Any
poor, well-drained soil will satisfy its needs.

Leontopodium alpinum (Edelweiss; Lions-Foot) hardy
peren., 5 to 7 inches

American tourists whose visits to Switzerland are disappointing because it's so difficult to obtain clearance for bringing
home plants can start Edelweiss from seed. Even without
bottom heat, it will germinate in ten days, and be ready to
bloom in about ten weeks. Its delightful foliage and ever-
lasting little blossoms make it a charmer for the year-round
light-garden. And if you want it in your outdoor rock garden,
start the seeds in February, give them a start under lights
when they have sprouted, set them out late in March, and
they should bloom all of the first season. They like gritty,
loose, dry soil, so don't overwater them in the light-garden.

Lobularia maritima (Sweet Alyssum) hardy annual or hardy
peren., 6 to 12 inches

This plant is not to be confused with Basket-of-Gold. Seeds

germinate in five days, and if started in December or January will be ready to set outdoors or to continue in the light-garden by the end of May. Tightly potted, they will not spread in the light-garden as they will outdoors, and will continue to bloom for a long time, starting in midsummer. Best under cool white and warm white lamp combination.

Majorana hortensis (Sweet Marjoram; *Origanum majoranum*) hardy annual, 1 to 2 feet

No herb garden is complete, indoors or out, without marjoram, and it is very easy to grow. Sow seeds one-half inch deep in vermiculite, about the first of March if you plan to set it outdoors to bloom in early summer. If you want to keep it permanently in the light-garden, for its spicy fragrance and its clusters of tiny white flowers, plan on bloom about twelve weeks after you sow the seeds. Transplant the seedlings into half loam, half sand, in which it will grow happily anywhere.

Marigolds (see *Tagetes*)

Mathiola bicornis (Night-scented Stock; Evening-scented Stock) hardy annual, 3 to 9 inches; and *Mathiola incana annua* (Ten-Weeks Stock) hardy annual, 6 to 12 inches or 12 to 24 inches

Choose your stock according to height if you care to, or try both, planting them at different times. They are all best propagated from seed, which normally germinates in five days if planted one-eighth inch deep in vermiculite. When the seedlings are large enough to handle, transplant into pots that can be kept permanently in the light-garden or moved back to the light-garden from outdoors before the first frost. Stock will not winter over in the outdoor garden, but can continue to bloom under lights if you bring the plants in early enough to prevent frosting.

Night-scented Stock is more interesting for its fragrance than for its bloom if you keep it permanently in the light-garden. As its name indicates, it blooms after the lights have been turned off, lasting through until the next noon, perfuming the light-garden area. Ten-Weeks Stock is so called because it takes about ten weeks from seed to bloom, which it does during the day. It, too, is delicately fragrant.

Stocks want a cool environment, and do best if your light-garden gets no warmer than 65° F. They also want extra attention to moisture (just tell yourself "I must water my stocks") and if the ordinary garden soil in which they are planted is on the acid side, add a teaspoonful of lime to each pot.

There is no reason why you can't have this very popular plant in bloom at all times in your light-garden. You can plant the seed at any time and expect the same growth cycle. For example, plant *M. bicornis* in November, put it in permanent pots under lights in December, and you should have bloom before March. Some plant growers have found that growing stock under lights weakens the stems but produces flowers earlier than those that are not given the light treatment, because it is a long-day plant and can take sixteen hours; but it is agreed that once the buds are formed, they will open into bloom earlier in the light-garden than without lights. If you set it outdoors, wait until the trees have leafed out. And don't hesitate to use your light-garden flowers as cutting flowers. Stock is only one of the many that you can grow indoors for cutting, and staggered sowing and production will always give you replacements for those plants that look a bit dreary after the flowers are cut.

Morning-Glory (see *Ipomoea*)

Oenothera caespitosa (Evening-Scented Primrose) hardy bien., 4 to 8 inches

You can purchase these plants, beg or steal suckers, divide

their roots, or take stem cuttings. Or you can propagate from seed, which you will probably want to do if you are intrigued by the stratification method of making biennials bloom in their first year. If seed is your choice, stratify them soon after Christmas in your ice-cube tray, as we have described in chapter 6. Keep them frozen until the end of January or the first week in February—four to six weeks. Then sow them in vermiculite, and when they have sprouted, set them under lights in sandy loam. They will bloom under light, but give off their best fragrance after the lights are turned off. Being short-day plants, they can be delightful fun when you put them onto your wheeled tray for plants that have had their ten hours under lights, move them into an unlighted area, and sniff. They like to be in a fairly dry atmosphere, so don't mist too much around them. Bloom outdoors in midsummer if set outdoors in early spring.

Origanum vulgare (Pot Marjoram; Wild Marjoram; Winter-Sweet) hardy peren., 15 to 30 inches

Nothing so well relieves the blandness of modern pre-fabricated meals as spices and herbs; and none is so spicy as those you have grown in your own herb garden. But in addition to teasing the jaded pallet, most herbs have cheerful blooms. Pot Marjoram is no exception, and is a delightful addition to your gourmet light-garden. It's really easiest to start with purchased plants—unless your neighbor gives you some when she divides hers, which she will do because they spread. However you acquire your plants, they need to be potted fairly tightly in ordinary garden soil if they are to stay indoors. Let the soil get thoroughly dry when you have potted them, then saturate it. While you are letting it dry out, keep it in shade, but when it is time to water it the first time after potting, set it close to the lights in your light-garden, or in a sunny spot outdoors. If it goes outdoors, leave it potted, because if you live north of Washington, D.C., you'll have to bring it indoors for the winter or lose it to the frost. In more southern climates, you can set it out in the fall as well as in spring, and it will winter over. It blooms in midsummer if set out as seedlings when the frost is gone from the ground.

Papaver nudicaule (Iceland Poppy) hardy peren., 8 to 12 inches

Everyone loves poppies, and this is one that will fit well in your permanent light-garden. Seeds germinate in ten days. Sow them in vermiculite-filled peat pots and feed them with plant food regularly after their first true leaves appears. Don't transplant them until the seedlings are six inches high unless their roots are protruding dangerously through the peat pots. Ideally, if they are to go outdoors, they should never have to be transplanted, since you merely dig a hole and set the peat pot into it. In the light-garden, if you know at sowing time that you are going to leave them there permanently, you can start them in their permanent containers. When they are six inches high, add a little peat moss to the vermiculite. They like a light, sandy loam with added humus outdoors, where they bloom from early summer to frost if you sow the seeds in December. Even though they are difficult to transplant, they can be propagated by taking off suckers or stolons from established plants, in the fall.

Pelargonium hybrids (Garden Geraniums) half-hardy peren., 12 to 20 inches

Growing geraniums to bloom under artificial light is a subject of much disagreement. So many studies have led to the conclusion that they will not bloom at all, that we have several times been tempted to say, "Those aren't geraniums that we have blooming in our light-garden." Yet we know that they are, and we are beginning to appreciate the fact that by trial and error we brought them to bloom under the rare combination of fluorescent lights that has proved successful for them in our light-garden.

One pioneer light-gardener said initially that geraniums grow easily under lights, but reported five years later that they can be brought to bloom only if you take them out from the light-garden and put them on the window sill when they show signs of budding. Another light-garden enthusiast reports that only Frau Berta Kamm can be brought into bloom under lights. (This variety is on the market only in very limited quantities.)

This variance in results of patient testing whets the appetite to try for the unusual and to look for a reason. The reason *may* be a matter of temperature. Both laboratory experiments and commercial crops indicate that geraniums grow best in a temperature that never falls below 55° F. although they will continue to live, without growing, through cold spells down to freezing.

In the Johnston light-garden, we have brought geraniums to bloom by the sheer coincidence of having combined fluorescent tubes that produce an abundance of light energy. We have done it with three different combinations, all in 40-watt tubes: a Power-Twist (described in chapter 2) in Candlelight color, combined with a cool white standard tube; a Power-Twist combined with a plant-growth tube; and a Power-Twist combined with a standard cool white lamp that has a built-in reflector (also described in chapter 2). Any one of these three combinations includes the Power-Twist, which doubles the light intensity of the same wattage in an ordinary tube; and the reflector tube also increases the effectiveness of the same wattage. So we conclude that geraniums need more intense light than most flowering plants. At any rate, we know that geraniums will bloom under artificial light, but perhaps not so well unless you give them an extra boost, both with added light intensity and warmer temperatures.

With this background information, we would suggest that you start your geraniums from purchased plants or from cuttings. When ours get leggy, we simply prune them and root the cuttings in vermiculite in the light-garden, where they quickly grow new roots and are ready to pot in a couple of weeks in ordinary soil. They are considered difficult to grow from seed, but not at all impossible. The seeming difficulty lies in the fact that they may or may not germinate in the anticipated fifteen days, so for the geranium experimenter, we recommend bottom heat for seeds. You can start them any time, and they will bloom when they are ready. Three-inch seedlings may take as long as a year, as ours did, even though they spent the summer outdoors. But once they begin to bloom, given the temperature and light that they like, they will bloom profusely for several months, then need a rest before they repeat. They like to have their soil become quite dry before watering, then thoroughly soaked. And when you take cuttings, be sure to discard the woody section and save only the fleshy stem for rooting. Pruning drastically close to the base of the major stem produces a flock of new shoots within a week or two, coming from both stem and roots. Geraniums are fun and challenging to the light-gardener. Those grown as outdoor bedding plants should be hardened off in mid-May, to be set out after Decoration Day.

Petunia hybrids (Petunia) hardy annual or half-hardy peren., 7 to 15 inches

On a long-day schedule, our petunias flower rapidly. But we have also grown them under short-day conditions, and they did eventually flower too. Petunias *can* be raised from seed, but it is sometimes a difficult and discouraging proposition. Being very fine seed, it must be sown only on top of the vermiculite without covering, and misted into secure position. Or you can mix it with sand, and scatter the sand on top of the growing medium, pressing it firmly. Start seeds in late February, and transplant seedlings into peat pots if they are to be set outdoors when the soil is warm. Put them under lights to grow sturdy, pinch out the central shoot to encourage bushiness, harden off in late April, and set them out in their peat pots in mid-May to bloom from midsummer until frost.

In 1963, a new variety of cascade petunia was sent to us for testing. Each of us received a dozen peat pots containing plants about three or four inches high, individually packed in clear plastic bags, tightly closed and beaded with moisture from the potted plant inside. Our packages reached the office on Monday, and neither of us had an opportunity to plant before the following weekend, so we set them, still enclosed in their opened plastic bags, into the Carrière light-garden to wait for transportation—one batch south to New Jersey by train; the other, north to Connecticut by car.

Before the week was out, we had lost several because they had obviously been too damp. Had we taken the plants from their plastic bags, they would have done well under lights, but late office hours are not compatible with careful gardening. It isn't always possible to put your plants into the ground when you acquire them, but it *is* possible to treat them respectfully and beneficially in your light-garden.

Incidentally, the cascade petunias that survived in our outdoor gardens did beautifully when brought into the light-garden before frost as potted plants, and are a distinct addition to any light-garden. Most petunias will continue to bloom under lights when moved from outdoors, but these are especially attractive because they hang so prettily over the pot rims, providing interest at a different eye level. Keep the flowers picked for continuing blooms, and if you want to experiment with seeds, sow seeds under light instead of in darkness.

Phlox drummondii (Annual Phlox; Drummond's Phlox; Texan Pride) hardy annual, 12 to 20 inches

Best grown from seed, which germinates normally in 10

days, sown in February. Sow them thinly so that thinning out the seedlings will be easier. Set the seedlings under lights in peat pots filled with ordinary soil, as they dislike transplanting. Set them outdoors from mid-May to the first of June, for bloom by the first of July. Or sow the seeds in August or September for midwinter bloom indoors in the light-garden. Often flower continuously for eight to ten weeks, and dwarf varieties are particularly attractive for the light-garden. Outdoors, they tend to self-sow, and you can bring in some from the outdoor garden simply by dividing them, or by taking root or stem cuttings. They prefer a cool location—below 60° F.—for best bloom, and although they are day-length-neutral, they can take fourteen to sixteen hours of garden lighting without flinching. A short-day schedule delays flowers, produces sturdier plants.

Pinks (see *Dianthus*)

Poppy (see *Eschscholtzia;* and *Papaver*)

Portulaca grandiflora (Rose Moss) hardy annual, 2 inches

In 1903 an article was published that cleared the air for all of us who talk to our plants. *"Of course* I talk to my plants" made us all feel more normal about what we suspect is the habit of all avid gardeners who recognize freedom of speech. The one we talk to most is "Porchie". Our portulacas are individuals, definitely people-plants, who close their little petals when a cloud hides the sun, and smile twinklingly whenever the light smiles upon them. All this and attractive foliage too. We remember searching in vain for the flower in a friend's garden, merely because it happened to be a somewhat overcast day, and "porchie" wasn't showing its face.

Most years we buy our plants, because germinating from seeds is something of a task, and we don't want to miss having portulacas. But if you put your glasses on, you can see the tiny seeds, which are easily gathered by collecting seed pods when you're picking off dead blooms in early fall. Mix them with sand, scatter the sand on top of the vermiculite in your seed tray, and spray with the mister. Don't cover with vermiculite, but of course, keep the moisture in with a plastic bag until they have sprouted. When they are large enough to handle, plant individual seedlings in peat pots, put them in the light-garden to grow sturdy, and when the soil is warm, you can set them outdoors to bloom from midsummer until frost.

Or you can keep them permanently in the light-garden, not more than six inches below the light tubes, directly under the center of the lamps. A pedestal container is good for this purpose, since it both confines them in their roots so that they won't spread too much, and lifts them closer to the lights. Their growth habit is such that they will be very showy, hanging over the edge of the container. Ordinary to sandy soil, kept fairly dry, will please them best. We dig ours up from the outdoor garden before frost, and bring them back to continue blooming under lights. The more light energy they receive, the more bloom you will see. Lamps with built-in reflectors are excellent for "porchies", and we have success with ordinary 40-watt fluorescents too.

Primrose (see *Oenothera*)

Rosmarinus officinalis (Rosemary) hardy peren., 36 inches

One of the less-known herbs for cookery, Rosemary is nevertheless a plant that should be included in the gourmet garden. Buy the plants if you have to, but you'll most likely find a friend who will give you stem cuttings to root in pots under lights at any time you happen to acquire them. It is not reliably hardy north of New York City, so you might as well plan on keeping it indoors permanently, with the possibility of setting out rooted stem cuttings into the summer garden.

You'll have plenty of stem cuttings, because in order to keep
its height within bounds, you'll need to prune it frequently.
Rosemary is a hardy evergreen shrub in the southland, and
doesn't in the least mind being pruned. It prefers poor soil,
well drained, and will be more fragrant if you don't fertilize
it.

Salvia officinalis (Garden Sage) hardy peren., 12 to 24 inches

Salvia pitcheri (Blue Sage) hardy peren., 48 to 60 inches; and

Salvia splendens (Red Sage; Red Salvia; Scarlet Sage), annual, 15 to 30 inches

The salvias are another of the delights of our gardens. The
annual red salvia is always the more spectacular, of course,
but the blue *Salvia officinalis* shows to advantage against a
tall line of white gladiolus, or planted close to its red relative. The dwarf varieties are especially delightful in the light-
garden, too.

We prefer to give the seeds bottom heat, since they sometimes take longer than their stated fifteen days without it, for
germination. We start them in moist vermiculite, and transplant when they are large enough to have leaves. In peat
pots or permanent containers, depending on whether they are
headed for the outdoor garden (peat pots) or to stay indoors,
they are happiest in a mixture of three-quarters good potting
soil and one-quarter sand, with room enough so that they will
not become potbound. When they are four inches high, we
pinch them back to make bushier growth. Being short-day
plants, they will do best in the permanent light-garden with
only ten hours of light. However, they will bloom eventually
on long-day schedule. And similarly, when set outdoors, they
will vegetate instead of blooming, until the days begin to
shorten. But once they have started to bloom, nothing but
the first frost will stop them. As we have said before, the first
frost always comes when you least expect it, and we have

found it wise to take stem cuttings soon after Labor Day, root them in vermiculite, and pot them up in the same mixture of potting soil and sand to which they have been accustomed. This ensures winter bloom, especially if we pinch them back for bushier growth.

One of our early experiences with salvia was when we sowed the seeds and started their growth in the office light-garden. They came to maturity in February, but failed to bloom under the 20 watts provided by the small planter we were testing. So we put them on a window sill that faces east and south, with sun coming in from about eight in the morning until noon. There, they bloomed profusely for six weeks, by which time the ground in Connecticut had warmed up, and we set them out in the outdoor garden there. No bloom, but much greenery developed—until August, when they suddenly burst forth in a riot of color that lasted until that inevitable surprise frost came in mid-September. Incidentally, that frost blackened the blooms and wilted the foliage, but in a week of balmy weather immediately afterward, new shoots came up from the roots, and a few buds that had somehow not responded to the touch of cold bloomed brightly.

Sedum acre (Wall Pepper; Golden Moss) hardy peren., 2 to 4 inches;

Sedum album (Worm-Grass) hardy peren., 4 to 6 inches;

Sedum sieboldi (Sedum) hardy peren., 8 to 12 inches; and

Sedum spectabile (Stonecrop) hardy peren., 12 to 20 inches

The sedums never fail to fascinate us, and in our stony, steeply sloping Connecticut garden, where grass is difficult to grow and rock gardens are a practical necessity to give support to leveled terrace beds, the sedums provide interesting contrast in texture, form and color—as well as being most obliging ground covers. So it naturally follows that the Carrière light-garden usually houses a few choice specimen plants of one kind of sedum or another. They are so easy to divide that we have never had to start them from seed. Our friends know our love for them, and keep us well supplied when their own plants creep out of hand. But they can be started from seed, which normally germinates in five days, and if started in February, for example, can be set out when the ground is ready for planting, to bloom—if bloom is important—at varying times in the summer.

The sedum that we enjoy most is *Sedum acre*. As usual, a neighbor handed us a handful last summer and said, "This grows like mad. It will probably be good for some of those corners where the round beds come together." Within a month, they had become so well established that we took stem cuttings and tucked them into some other difficult places. They grow clinging little roots from almost any part of the tiny stem that touches a growing medium and get a good start in vermiculite. When autumn came, our spoon-holder planter in the kitchen had need of replanting, so we cleaned out the tired old soil and dead roots of philodendron, lined it with a fresh sheet of Saran Wrap, and planted *Sedum acre* in it. Two weeks before Christmas we used this planter box as a source of supply, took stem cuttings again, planted them in a little hanging basket, and hung them in the light-garden to take root. They made a most delightful little Christmas gift, having responded beautifully to the light-garden treatment.

Sedums prefer sandy loam, don't in the least mind stones, want occasional water but no wet feet, and will actually come back to life from a water-starved diet of a month without watering, if they have not been in too warm a temperature. We do not recommend this neglectful procedure, but were so pleased that ours revived that we want to pass on this ray of hope to others who may have to be away from their plants longer than expected.

Sempervivum tectorum (Houseleek; Hen-and-Chickens; Roof Houseleek: Old-Man-and-Woman) hardy peren., 3 to 12 inches

Except for the fact that this one germinates from seed a little slower (fifteen days) it is treated like the sedums. But the easier way to start a flock in your light-garden is to buy the plants or have them given to you. They send out stolons that take root close to the parent (hen) and become small reproductions (chickens), which can be divided readily and transplanted anywhere. Poor soil and good drainage are needed, and once your flock is established, you'll want to keep it confined in a container for light-garden residence, to check its tendency to spread. Planted in a container that has texture— a clay pot, a wooden box, or anything to which the roots can cling, the plants will have an opportunity to mound over the edge and cascade attractively down the sides.

Shasta Daisy (see *Chrysanthemum maximum*)

Snapdragon (see *Antirrhinum*)

Stock (see *Mathiola*)

Sunflower (see *Helianthus*)

Sweet William (see *Dianthus*)

Tagetes erecta (African Marigold) hardy annual, 8 to 24 inches; and

Tagetes patula (French Marigold) hardy annual, 7 to 12 inches

Dwarf marigolds are one of the mainstays of our light-gardens in the winter, and of our outdoor gardens in the summer. Easy to grow from seed, always gay and colorful when blooming, they're even fun to use as greenery before they blossom, because their foliage is interestingly ragged and makes a good dark-green foil for taller plants that are in bloom in the light-garden.

We always start ours from seed, frequently exchanging seed pods with friends and each other as we pick them off in the autumn to keep new flowers blooming through the first of the frosts. Planted about one-quarter inch deep in moist vermiculite and given bottom heat and darkness for germination, we have found sprouts showing twenty-four hours later, although the seeds are normally supposed to take five days before they sprout. If given the short-day treatment of no more than ten hours in the light-garden, they can bloom in about fifteen weeks from the time you sow the seeds. We like to stagger the seed sowing, starting in January, so that we will have the gay little flowers constantly on hand in the light-garden, and a sufficient supply to be set out in our outdoor borders and rock gardens when the trees have leafed out. Outdoors, being short-day plants, they normally bloom from July until frost. But by bringing them to the blooming stage in the light-garden and then carefully choosing an outdoor location where trees shade them a little, providing the equivalent of a short day, we have had outdoor bloom as early as June.

And in the fall, when we have gathered seeds and dried them out for a couple of weeks, we plant them in the usual way to grow and bloom in the light-garden by Christmastime. They do well in average soil, and outgrow their dwarf habits if fed with too much prepared manure as fertilizer. In an outdoor garden on the eastern end of Long Island, where everything grows lushly, they grew so abundantly that they were almost a nuisance, because "too many cooks" had applied fertilizer to the flower beds. They need good air circulation around their stems, and a reasonable supply of moisture without waterlogging the roots.

Thymus vulgaria (Thyme) hardy peren., 6 to 8 inches

Thyme is another of the "musts" for the gourmet garden, and if your plant-exchanging friends don't share theirs with you, you can purchase the plants or start them from seed. Although the flowers are of minor importance, they are attractive, and should appear in June if you start your seeds in January. For the herb garden under lights, start the seeds at any convenient time. Sow on top of soaked vermiculite without a covering layer. They are very strong. Transplant the seedlings into poor, well-drained soil, and count on having deliciously scented plants for two or three years. They tend to die out after a few years, so prepare to replace them by collecting seeds after bloom in the second year, so that you can have well-started replacements on hand when you need them.

Verbena hortensis (Garden Verbena; Vervain) half-hardy peren., 5 to 8 inches or 8 to 12 inches

We prefer the dwarf type, which is one of our most pleasing light-garden plants. Seeds sown in January with bottom heat should produce bloom by July. They prefer a cool temperature of 60° to 65° F. until they are well established, and we find they do best in our light-garden under a combination of 40-watt Power-Twist and 40-watt plant-growth lamps, long day. In our outdoor area, they may not be more than annuals unless they are set out in pots and brought back into the light-garden for continued bloom before frost can damage them.

Zinnia hybrids (Zinnia; Youth-and-Old-Age; Cut-and-Come-Again) half-hardy annual, 8 to 15 inches or 18 to 30 inches

Zinnia seeds germinate normally in five days, and we start them in February for our own and our neighbors' gardens.

We sow them one-eighth inch deep in moist vermiculite, and when they are large enough to handle, transplant them into peat pots in good loam, one to a pot. They then take no more than ten hours of artificial light a day, because they are short-day plants and will flower much faster if treated this way. They must be watered carefully and slowly, letting the moisture seep in and become absorbed by the soil, never accumulating around the stems on top. Outdoors, they will bloom in June with a light-garden start.

We like to keep some permanently in the light-garden, and we leave the side shoots on these plants, which then produce smaller flowers but bushier growth. For the outdoor plants, in order to have large single blooms, we nip off the side shoots. And sometimes we reserve some of the seeds for sowing in June, to have them in bloom in the light-garden from autumn through winter.

Plants for Less Intense Light

The plants that follow will grow best in less intense light. They *can* be placed on the front or back edge of your light-garden table where the light is about the same intensity as it is at both ends of the tubes or on the floor away from maximum light.

Plants that grow outdoors in partial shade are excellent for use at the front, back or end zones of the garden.

If the plants stretch upward, growing too long between the nodes, they are asking to be put a little closer to the light. If they lean away from the light source, move them farther out from the center. And of course, if they lean toward it, move them in a little. We usually start shade-loving plants about twelve inches away from the bottom of the tubes, and move them up only if they indicate that they need more light.

There are so many gradations of "partial shade" in the outdoor garden that only experimentation in the light-garden can indicate exact placement for individual plants, even within the general rules that apply to the species and varieties.

Ageratum houstonianum (Ageratum; Floss-Flower) half-hardy annual, 5 to 7 inches

Seeds germinate normally within five days, and if sown in February should be ready to bloom in June. Sow them in vermiculite, and when they are large enough to handle, transplant into individual peat pots filled with ordinary potting soil. Place them along the front or back edge of the light-garden area in the center, about twelve inches below the bottom of the lamps. By the time the outdoor soil is warm, they will be sturdy enough to set out. We like to start some of the seeds in September, to provide a touch of blue in the winter light-garden, too.

Ajuga genevensis (Bugleweed) peren., 6 to 10 inches

Best started from cuttings, this foliage plant is interesting and adaptable in the light-garden. Cuttings are easy to find if you know anyone who has *Ajuga*, because it spreads profusely as an outdoor ground cover (don't say we didn't warn you) and if kept in pots, will need repotting about once a year or it will die of overcrowding. We have found it a delightful plant for the light-garden, because it seems to do well wherever we feel the need for an interestingly textured and colored underlining of foliage. We move it from side to side, from front to back, sometimes in the center, sometimes in a corner, and wherever it goes, so long as it is not directly under the tubes, it flourishes.

Amaryllis, 12 to 24 inches

If you start with really fresh seed, you can have an Amaryllis blooming in two years. But it's much easier to start with prepared bulbs purchased in September to bloom in two months. Pot the bulb immediately with an inch of soil around it on all sides. (If it's a five-inch bulb, use a seven-inch pot.) Keep the soil loose, and mix a little peat moss into it. Plant the bulb so that its upper one-third is exposed. Water it well at planting time, then sparingly thereafter. It likes moisture but resents being too wet. When potted, place it about eight inches under one end of your fluorescent tubes, and leave it there until it buds.

When the plant is about to bloom, move it to the center of the shelf, directly under the light source, water it often and feed it regularly. After it has flowered, cut off the dead bloom and keep the plant under the lights until the foliage has died down. Then it can be put outdoors in a shady place, or dried off and stored in a cool temperature where it is dark and dry. Bring it in from outdoors before frost, or take it out of its storage place at the end of two months, replant, and water it back to wakefulness and activity as before. Be careful not to disturb the roots any more than necessary when you remove the offsets from the mature bulb.

Anthurium Schwerzerianum; and A. *veitchi*, (Flamingo Plant) 24 to 36 inches

Anthurium veitchi is best known for its foliage, but A. *Schwerzerianum* is the variety that most collectors grow, for its spectacular, very long-lasting bloom. Its culture is somewhat similar to that of Cattleya orchids. If you don't have a propagating case, its easiest to buy your first plant, and later propagate by division or suckers broken off the plant and rooted in vermiculite with bottom heat. The plants like warmth and plenty of humidity. Once they have established roots, pot them in osmunda and add milled sphagnum moss as the roots grow, in order to keep them thoroughly moist. Be sure to provide good drainage.

When the buds begin to form, start fertilizing regularly, and keep the plant warm but well off-centered from the light source. It takes up a lot of space in a light-garden, and since it does not want direct light for flowering, it can be set close to the light-garden in a nearby corner as accent for the more light-preferring plants.

Give it a rest in the summer in a cool place—it can have its pot plunged into a shady spot in the outdoor garden—and bring it back indoors before the weather turns cool.

Aquilegia chrysanthea (Columbine) hardy peren., 24 to 36 inches

Seeds normally germinate slowly, but if you supply bottom heat under the vermiculite, you should have sprouts in fifteen days. Start them in February in vermiculite, pot the seedlings in a good, medium-light soil, and set them about twelve inches below the light source, front, back or sides. Let them grow slowly so that they will become really sturdy, and set them outdoors when they are eight to ten inches tall. They want plenty of moisture, and will grow where the shade is very light. In the light-garden, because they are tall plants, they can be kept in the corners. If you wish, you can dig them from the outdoor garden after a good frost in the fall, pot them up, and give them a light-garden beginning before the following outdoor season begins. This is suggested largely because they tend to die out in three or four years, and you may want to have replacements for your older plants.

Aubretia deltoidea (Purple Rock Cress) hardy peren., 3 to 6 inches

This attractive little rock-garden plant tends to die out in a few years, and if you like it as well as we do, you'll want to have replacements. So take stem cuttings or divide your clump in June or whenever your plants have finished their early-spring bloom, root cuttings from them in vermiculite until the roots are well established, and then pot them in half sand and half loam. Keep them moist, placed ten to twelve inches beneath the ends of the lamps. They like fairly short days, and should not have more than eleven or twelve hours of lighting. Plants set outdoors in October will bloom the following spring. Like sandy soil, well drained.

Azalea

It is possible to make your gift plant bloom again. When you receive it, put it directly under the center of the tubes and keep it there until it flowers. When it begins to flower, move it to the end zone or off-centered under the light-garden. Azaleas prefer rainwater, but do not like to be water-logged. They should not be exposed to gas fumes, as they are very

sensitive. Keep your plant in a fairly cool temperature. To
have repeated blooming periods, keep the pot watered until
mid-May, then set it into the outdoor garden. Prune back
long shoots to keep the plant shapely, and feed it every few
weeks with fertilizer. In the fall, after a few weeks of cool
weather, bring the plant indoors and keep it at 65° F. In
November, place it directly under the lights in the light-
garden until it flowers again.

Begonia

Tuberous-rooted, fibrous-rooted, and rhizomatous begonias
are all popular house plants. Members of the Begonia Society
tell us that all varieties are being grown successfully under
artificial light. Most difficult type appears to be the tuberous,
but it can be done. Society members often start begonias
from seed, and we have included seeding among the propagation methods. The seeds are very fine, and are best propagated by sowing on the top of the growing medium, pressed
in, sprayed with water, and not covered with a top layer.
Give them bottom heat.

Tuberous-rooted types bloom in six months from seed
started in December or January. Seed sometimes takes three
weeks to germinate. They are dormant during the late fall
and early winter. These are long-day plants, and need sixteen hours under the light, about 6 inches below the center
of the tubes. Soil should be rich and acid, including some
leafmold, with good drainage. They want high humidity.

You can also propagate them by dividing the mature (two
year-old) tubers, making sure that each segment has its own
red bud included. For continuous bloom, stagger plantings
from January through May. The tubers should be planted,
concave side up, and pressed into the planting medium so
that they are a little below the top level, but not covered.
When four inches tall, transplant into porous, well-drained
soil, and keep moist. Give them small feedings, and stop wa-

tering when bloom is finished. Then dry out the tubers, store in a dark, dry place until February or March. Outdoors, they can be set into a shady place and kept moist during the summer, brought in before there is any danger of frost.

Fibrous-rooted begonia (including *Semperflorens,* Wax; Rose—which are all the same) bloom from seed in four to six months, and may be pinched back if they get leggy. They are the easiest begonias to grow under lights (except the Calla Lily variety, which is temperamental and difficult). Dwarf, compact, almost everblooming, they are ideal light-garden residents for several years, except for the Christmas begonia, which blooms its utmost in one year and is best discarded after it has bloomed.

Fibrous-rooted begonias are best rooted from leaf cuttings, as illustrated and described in chapter 6. But grown from seed, they will germinate in ten days, to bloom in four to six months. They provide both upright and trailing varieties.

Rhizomatous begonias withstand hot, dry house atmosphere better than the other varieties. All they ask is that the air be fresh and moist around them. Keep them off-centered in the light-garden, under the ends of tubes or on the edges of shelves. In this group, the Rex is probably the most popular. They are dormant in winter, and put on their best foliage show in May through August, except for Merry Christmas and Queen of Hanover, which bloom in winter. Begonias do best in the light-garden if kept close under the light (about six inches below) for a long day. At least one Begonia Society member we know adds high-voltage incandescent lamps to his fluorescents to make the plants bloom sooner. We have had spectacular success with the cascade begonias, new in 1963, which we brought to bloom under lights and hung in baskets in our outdoor gardens. Before winter, we brought them back indoors, where they continued to bloom.

Bellis perennis (English daisy; Bachelors-Button) hardy
peren., 4 to 6 inches

This is *the* English daisy, and a charmer for the permanent
light-garden or for outdoors. Seeds germinate in eight days,
but if you're in a hurry, give them bottom heat. Sow them
one-eighth inch deep in February, transplant the seedlings
into potting soil and keep the atmosphere moist around them.
Place them about eight inches below the tubes at the tube
ends, and they should be in bloom from early summer on into
autumn. They may want a short rest period before they begin
to bloom again, but their foliage is pretty even when they
are not blooming. You can also bring them in from your outdoor garden by division; or sow some of the seeds in August
for bloom in very early spring. They do best, of course, in the
sort of cool, moist atmosphere that is typical of their native
England, and if you live in the South, you may not find them
too successful outdoors. Flowers are best on a long-day schedule, but plants (six to eight weeks after seeds are planted)
develop better form on short day.

Bromeliads

Most bromeliads, like orchids, have developed aerial roots
so that they can cling to rocks and trees in their native habitat. But they can also be grown in soil if their roots are not
allowed to rot from excess water. They take most of their
nourishment through their leaves, and some bromeliads have
been known to thrive even after the entire root system had
been removed.

They respond well to light-garden residence, and lend
themselves to a large variety of interesting arrangements.
One of our bromeliad-fan friends makes living pictures of
them in fluorescent-lighted picture frames.

Easy to care for if potted in light, porous soil (some prefer
osmunda), they need a little water occasionally poured into
the soil, but most of the watering should go directly into the

center of the plant. Each plant has a little cup in its center, and the cup must be kept filled with fresh water. They take the water in slowly, however, and can be left confidently while you go away for a two-week vacation if you take care of them first this way: Fill the plant cup, and put a clear plastic bag over the plant, pulling it down so that it is closed tightly around the pot bottom. This will hold the moisture and the plant will be quite content without further attention until you return.

Bromeliads, which include the pineapple, flower only once, then die. But the flower remains in bloom for months, and the plant puts forth new little plants around its base, so that you can divide them, pot them individually, and continue your enjoyment of the same variety of bromelliad. New plants blossom within a year or two. They are difficult to start from seed, even if you provide bottom heat.

Among the most popular bromeliads are *Ananas* (pineapple); *Aechmea* (Urn plant); *Bilbergias* (Vase plant); *Cryptanthus* (Starfish plant); *Neoregelia* (Fingernail plant); *Tillandsia* (Spanish moss); and *Vriesea* (Flaming sword).

Caladium bicolor (Fancy-Leafed Caladium) peren., 1 to 2½ feet

Caladiums are started from tubers or bulblets or division of tubers, set into a rooting medium any time after the first of February. Rooting should follow their dormant period, which is a two- or three-month interval during the winter. They are excellent house plants, equally good in the outdoor garden. In either place, they can use intense light to keep them from turning green. They can spend some time in end zones if more convenient. If they begin to turn green instead of variegated, give them closer proximity to the light, because they are searching for the energy that only light can give them. Soil should be loam with leafmold added, with sand; or one-third each peat, soil, and sand. It must provide good drainage, and they must have high humidity in a warm temperature. Even when storing the bulbs during their dormancy, put them in a dry, warm place.

Calceolaria crenatiflora (Slipperwort; Satchel Plant)

This is another temporary house plant. Buy it or receive it as a gift, let it live until it's finished blooming, and don't try to propagate it. Since it should be sheltered from direct sunlight, you will naturally keep it in the end zone or on the shelf edges. It does not like to be overwatered, and if you pick off the dead blooms, it will continue to bloom for a longer period whenever you have it—which is usually at Christmas or Eastertime. Don't feed it, since you're not going to keep it. Keep the soil cool, and don't let water settle on its leaves.

Citrus (Orange, lemon, grapefruit, etc.)

Kids love to plant their fruit seeds, and these seeds are very obliging. Sow them as soon as they are ripe, soaking them overnight and covering one-half inch deep in the rooting medium. In five to seven weeks, you will have a little plant. Don't let the youngsters expect to pick fruit from these little plants, because they probably won't produce any unless pollinated when mature. But they're fun to watch because they grow quickly, placed under the center of the fluorescent tubes, about six inches below. They should be watered well until sprouted, and their normal bloom period is February and during the summer. They are unparticular as to soil, and very easy to grow in the light-garden.

Coleus (Painted Nettle)

No matter how your thumbs refuse to be green, you can grow coleus in your light-garden. As we write this paragraph, we see the five pots of coleus that resulted from a few sprigs of very weary-looking, pale, leggy stems that we nipped from plants on a New York window sill a month ago. In our light-garden, they are brilliantly colorful, and have been divided twice since we planted them in plain water to take root.

If you start coleus from seeds, use bottom heat, sow from March to May, and don't cover the tiny seeds with additional vermiculite. Just press them into place and mist water over them. Eventually, they will start to produce a very insignificant series of tiny blue blossoms on a long spike. Since it is not attractive and saps the strength from the brilliant foliage, nip it off as soon as you see it coming. Also, prune the plants as drastically as needed to keep them shapely, and of course, root the cuttings.

We keep our coleus in wall-brackets on the periphery of the light-garden, or in pots placed under the ends of the tubes or on edges of the shelves, where they do not receive such direct light that they blanche into pale colors. They are thirsty, and need well-drained rich loam kept moist at all times.

Cyperus alternifolius (Umbrella Plant) 24 to 48 inches

This is a tall one that can be used in the corners or on the floor close to the light-garden. It is a grassy water plant, and wants its roots kept very moist. It roots readily in water, like the coleus, or you can propagate by detaching a crown and rooting it in vermiculite.

Cytisus canariensis (Genista; Broom)

Genistas are grown from soft-wood cuttings taken from December to February or from July to October, given bottom heat in a cool atmosphere for rooting. They are kept in the light-garden under the ends of the tubes or on the shelf edges, moving them farther away when they bloom in early or late spring. They like high humidity, cool temperature, and plenty of water.

Digitalis purpurea (Foxglove) hardy bien., 24 to 48 inches

Seeds sown in December should produce bloom the following June. Sow them one-eighth inch deep in vermiculite, and
when they are large enough to handle, plant the individual
seedlings in peat pots filled with three-quarters garden loam
and one-quarter sand, thoroughly mixed. They dislike heat
and dryness, so try to keep them on the cool side and in a
moist atmosphere, placed about ten inches under the ends
of the lamps. They can be set outdoors when the leaves appear on the trees. Since they tend to die out after a few
years, you may want to divide them in August to be brought
back into the light-garden for replacements the following
year. Or you can start the seeds in August or September, to
have earlier bloom the following year outdoors.

Dionaea muscipula (Venus Flytrap)

The insect-eating plants are always oddities, and this one is
popular. If you have no insects, feed it tiny bits of ham-
burger, uncooked, but *never* give it plant food. It likes
warmth, humidity, and a place close under the center of the
lights (about six inches) with a cover over it to keep it humid.
Three inches of peat moss, sphagnum moss, vermiculite, or
perlite will hold its roots, and must be kept *always wet*. A
fish bowl or a brandy snifter covered with glass or plastic
will make a good home for it when it gets too big for the little
aluminum tray in which it usually is purchased. If you should
take it outdoors, uncover it but keep it in a very warm, sunny
place and be sure it is constantly wet.

Episcia

One gesneriad grower says that you shouldn't attempt Episcia
until you have convinced yourself you are successful with
African violets. But these plants are close cousins, and react

the same. Both are very easy to cultivate under lights, if kept about eleven inches below the ends of the fluorescent tubes where they are not over-energized by the lights. Episcia is excellent for the hanging basket, and therefore is good for light-garden corners. It wants warmth, shade, and humidity, with plenty of water in its well-drained soil. It is propagated by leaf cuttings, which we have described in chapter 6.

Ficus elastica (Rubber Plant)

Don't shudder—the modern Rubber Plant is much more attractive than the Victorian type, and is back in popularity again. It likes a warm, humid atmosphere without being over-watered, and if you have the upright type, better place it outside the light-garden where it gets only a bit of the light, because it's too tall to fit under the tubes and is a part-shade plant by nature. It will do well in the corner of a light-garden as background for other plants, too. If it becomes too leggy, prune it; and if it grows completely out of bounds, discard it. In its native habitat it grows to 100 feet. There are varieties that climb, and that are good for the walls of your light-garden—if you choose those that have small leaves instead of those that have leaves a foot wide and a foot and a half long. Just be careful that you don't have to cut holes in the ceilings to accommodate your plant.

Freesia

Hanging baskets are popular decorations indoors and out, and freesia will do well in a hanging basket in the light-garden or in a shaded area outdoors. It must be kept cool, and does not require direct sunlight or strong light intensity. Hang it in the corners of your light-garden, or outside the light-garden where it will become a part of the framing for the picture. It blooms for two to three months in the winter, if started in October.

Offsets or seeds can be staggered in the sowing so that you achieve longer blooming periods. Water well when they are growing, and you will have blooms within 3 months after planting. After it has flowered, gradually dry it off, shake out the corms, store them in a dry, cool place, and rest them for the summer.

Fuchsia

Much like Freesia, Fuchsia is excellent for hanging baskets and wants the same type of culture. Keep it cool and humid in light soil, give it a winter rest with very little water, and revive it in March with steady watering and increased warmth. It can be propagated from cuttings, and will do well either in the peripheral areas of the light-garden or outdoors in shade after danger of frost is past. To wake it into energetic activity and eventual bloom, put it under the more intense light of the center of the light-garden, about a foot below, until it shows signs of budding.

Gardenia

If you can devote your entire time to your light-garden babies every day, you may enjoy trying the temperamental gardenia. But be prepared to treat it with the utmost attention, spraying it with rain water four times every day without fail—only to have it refuse to bloom even when it's in bud. Undoubtedly, someone will say "But I've grown gardenias for years and never had any problem." Bless you. There *are* gardenias who *do* like people and behave appreciatively.

The gardenia wants acid soil, consisting of half peat and half sand. It wants no drafts or sudden changes in temperature. It wants dense humidity, regular feeding, with no water spilled on its foliage. It should not be allowed to become potbound. It is particularly susceptible to gases of all kinds, and wants to have the air around it sprayed three or four times every day without fail, with nothing but rainwater.

If you're still not discouraged, take cuttings of soft wood from December to February, root them for three to four weeks with lots of humidity and bottom heat, continuing the bottom heat through the first few months of life for the rooted cuttings. When it will bloom is a matter of conjecture, but it may do so. Being a short-day plant, it should be kept in the light-garden no more than 10 hours a day, under the ends of the lamps.

Hedera Helix (Hedera; English Ivy)

Ivies don't care in the least whether they have light or shade, but they are delightful in the corners of a light-garden or planted several in a pot to hang from a basket. Just keep them out of the range of the strongest light intensity, keep them relatively cool with high humidity, and spray their foliage free of dust. In August or September, you can acquire cuttings easily from outdoor plants, and if you are taking them from indoor plants, the best time is in December or January. They will root in water.

Helleborus niger (Christmas Rose; Winter Rose; Lenten Rose) hardy peren., 5 to 8 inches

A few of the difficult plants are fun to try, and the Christmas Rose is one in this category. Seeds may not germinate for six to nine months, and it will be eighteen months from seed-sowing to bloom. But if you want to start it from seeds, plant them individually one-quarter inch deep in peat pots as soon as fresh seeds are available, which is usually sometime in midsummer. Keep them moist, and when they have finally established themselves as sturdy little plants, set them outdoors in a shaded spot that you will be able to see easily in midwinter even if there is a foot of snow on the ground—because they bloom in December, January, or February, sometimes even blooming under the snow. They like moisture, but not wet feet.

The relatively easier way to propagate Christmas Roses is by division in late spring or early fall, but again, you have to be careful. The roots are very easily broken, and the plant resents transplanting. In the permanent light-garden, it needs short-day treatment of no more than ten hours lighting each day, and a cool atmosphere. Place it under an end of the lamp, about twelve inches below.

Helxine soleiroli (Baby tears; Mind Your Own Business)

So shy is this little plant that it grows happily where no light reaches it at all. It is an excellent ground cover for large potted plants that reach up and spread out, shading the soil of their pots but not covering it from view. It's also good for low bowls and for baskets, but it must be kept as far away from the light source as possible.

Impatiens balsamina (Golden Balsam; Impatiens; Patience; Lady's Slipper) half-hardy peren., 12 to 24 inches.

Seeds normally germinate in fifteen days, and will bloom in about four months. When you can handle the seedlings, transplant them from the vermiculite into individual peat pots filled with rich soil, and prepare to feed these hungry babies. They are gross feeders until they bloom, and they want moist soil, so don't neglect to add fertilizer to the water each time you water them. When the outdoor soil is warm, set them out. If you started the seeds in March, you should have bloom all summer long until the first frost, which will kill them. Because they do so well in the light-garden, blooming all winter, we carefully dig ours up before there is a chance of frost, bring them indoors, and keep them about eight inches below the ends of the fluorescents. Keeping the blooms picked as they fade will ensure continuous new blossoms, and pruning them makes them more compact.

Kalanchoe

This obliging plant shrugs off the dry air of a city apartment, and cheerfully blooms at Christmastime and once again, later in the season. The Tom Thumb or Vulcan varieties are best for potting in the light-garden, because they are small enough to fit under the lights, where they like to be centered and fairly close for ten hours a day, until they bloom. When the buds are set, move the plants to the edges of the shelves so they will not receive so much direct light. Propagation is by rooting the little plants that form around the margins of the leaves.

Lunaria annua (Honesty; Satinpod; Moonwort) hardy annual, 18 to 30 inches

A favorite for the dried-flower arranger, Lunaria is a fun plant. Seeds germinate in ten days, and for bloom the following summer, should be started in December. Since it resents transplanting, it's best to sow the seeds in one-inch peat pots about three to a pot, and thin out the weaklings when they have established roots. By putting them into vermiculite in the tiny pots, you can avoid the hazards of transplanting by setting the original peat pots into larger ones filled with good potting soil, placed eight inches under the ends of the fluorescents. Set them outdoors when the soil is warm, and after their fairly unimportant blooms in June or July, the seed pods for which they are valued will form. This is a plant that usually self-sows, once established in an outdoor location it likes. But just in case it shouldn't, you may want to pick a few seed pods, dry them, and plant them as before, for replacements to be set out next year.

Lupinus hybrids (Lupine), hardy annual, 12 to 20 inches

Unless you know certainly that the seeds are fresh, soak them before sowing one-quarter inch deep in vermiculite about seven months before you want them to bloom. Staggered sowings will provide early bloom that continues well into the fall in the outdoor garden, or can keep you constantly supplied with bloom in the permanent light-garden. These plants resent transplanting, but because their roots won't cling to vermiculite, it's safe to start them in vermiculite-filled trays. But when they are large enough to handle, set them into peat pots filled with sandy, enriched soil on the alkaline side, with vermiculite on the bottom for good drainage, and don't overwater them. Set them about ten inches under the ends of the fluorescents or centered on the front or back shelf edge, and as they grow taller in their center spikes, leave them in the same position, as they need more light as they mature. For compact plants to be kept in the light-garden, prune the center spike out. Even if they are bound for outdoors, this is good procedure to strengthen the roots. Keep them cool, and remove the old blooms as they fade, so that new ones will open.

Myosotis scorpiodoides (Forget-Me-Not), peren., 2 inches

Seeds normally germinate in a week or two, but with bottom heat, they'll sprout faster. Nothing is easier to grow, and you can have their delightful little blue accent in the light-garden at all times if you stagger your seed sowing—or take stem cuttings in March to increase the flock. The early varieties bloom in three months from the time you sow the seeds; later varieties may take five months. Sow the seeds one-quarter inch deep in moist vermiculite, transplant when you can handle the seedlings to rich garden loam, and keep them very moist but avoid letting water stand on their foliage. Feed them regularly as you water them. They should be placed about eight inches below the lights, and we like them on the front edge of the shelf for an underlining to taller, more light-loving plants. Flowers best on long-day but growing seedlings under short-day schedule delays flowers, produces good short-stemmed plants.

Orchids

The ever-increasing numbers of orchid-growing hobbyists are inevitably equipping their orchid greenhouses or cases with fluorescent lights, because these plants need carefully controlled light, humidity, and warmth. They are shade-loving plants but are also in the small group of plants that bloom best if they receive the extra stimulus of infra-red light. It is probable that when the use of high-voltage incandescents becomes widespread, these cool-burning bulbs will be included in light-gardens that are designed for orchids. Rule of thumb is 10 watts of incandescent light for each 40 watts of fluorescent. This addition is easily made to the light-garden by placing incandescent bulb sockets between the tubes of a double fluorescent setup, one socket at each end about one foot in from the extreme end of the fixture.

Orchid growers tell us that the plants do best if set very close to the light source—no more than two or three inches below the tubes. Although orchids differ according to genera in their requirements for temperature, light, humidity, and moisture, they are much more adaptable than their reputation indicates. They will adjust and live happily together much more readily than might be supposed.

The beginning orchid grower without experience would do well to start his collection with some of the less expensive varieties of Cypripedium, Cattleya, Phalaenopsis, or Oncidium. They are easier to grow than some of the others. Start with purchased plants, because propagation is an art in itself, and once you have become an orchid enthusiast, you will undoubtedly join up with others whose experience will help you. Propagation by seed is fascinating, but a job for the professional expert. Propagation by division is the method used by most orchid hobbyists to increase their collections.

Division is done when the plants need repotting, every two or three years, after they have finished their blooming period and become dormant.

Orchids need a great deal of humidity in the air around them, and in a hot atmosphere, need to be sprayed, but without allowing water to accumulate on their foliage. Their growing medium, which is osmunda for some varieties, must be kept constantly moist without overwatering except during the dormant period after flowering. Wardian cases or some form of glass or plastic enclosure are essential to holding the moisture around the plants, but ventilation must also be provided and carefully controlled. Automatic controls are useful in growing orchids, and especially important in providing the moisture they need if you can't tend them yourself every day at least once or twice.

Orchids are subject to attack by mealy bugs. To rid them of these pests, wipe the bugs off with cotton dipped in alcohol. A cue tip is good for this purpose.

Peperomia Cordata

This is another of the house plants that needs so little light energy that it can be placed outside the light-garden or used decoratively in the very peripheral areas. P. *glabella* is good for trailing over the edges of containers in which large plants are growing, exposing uninteresting potting soil to view. Or it can be planted in a hanging basket to decorate a corner of the light-garden. These plants need to be kept on the dry side, with very good drainage, as they are subject to root rot. The variegated types can use more light than the all-green plants, and if variegated leaves begin to turn green, move them closer to the light source. Keep the plants pruned back to shapeliness, and root the cuttings to increase the collection.

Saintpaulia (African Violet)

Although African violets can be grown very successfully on a filtered-sun window sill, or even on a table where a reading lamp gives them indirect light, it has become accepted practice to grow them under fluorescent lamps. Reason for this practice is that they will double or triple their flower production if given the correct position in the light-garden. Being shade-loving plants, they need to be placed under the ends of the fluorescent tubes, or on the edges of the shelves, eight to twelve inches below the lights. We find that they thrive best under a combination of plant-growth fluorescents with either warm white or daylight standard fluorescents, for twelve to sixteen hours. They are long-day plants, but too much light will make the foliage curl down over the edge of the container, in an effort to shield itself. One expert says that *Saintpaulias* grown under plant-growth fluorescents only can do with only fourteen hours of light. Too little light will make the stems grow long and spindly, keep the leaves pale, and the blooms sparse. Experimentation will tell you what your individual plants respond to best.

African violets want at least 50 percent relative humidity, and careful watering. The plants will tell you when to water. If the surface of the soil is dry to the touch, it's time to water. In doing so, be careful not to allow water to drop on the foliage, because each drop acts as a magnifying glass and can cause a burn as the light strikes it. Contrary to the opinion of many fanciers, these plants do not need to be watered only from their saucers through the bottom of the pots. They can be watered from the top, and even if it is your custom to pour water into the saucers, they should occasionally be watered from the top to wash the salts down through the soil. But always use room-temperature water, or a little warmer, and a watering can with a long spout that will reach under the foliage, to avoid spotting it. Single-bloom plants like their water in small doses, more frequently applied than for double-bloom plants.

Propagation is usually done by leaf cuttings or by division of crowns, which can be divided about every six months. Leaf cutting is described and illustrated in chapter 6. A healthy leaf can be rooted in plain water or in vermiculite, and if you are rooting several at the same time, support them so that they do not touch each other. When the roots are about an inch long, which will be within ten weeks, they are ready to plant in loose, porous soil. Equal parts of potting soil, sand, and peat are recommended, or the potting soil commercially packaged specifically for African violets, a little more acid than average potting soil, can be used. Cover the cuttings with plastic bags to keep the moisture around them, and place them in the light-garden about six inches under the ends of the tubes, for faster rooting. They will become flowering plants from leaf cuttings in eight to ten months; from seed, in six or seven months.

They need a free circulation of air around them, and a warm temperature of 65 to 70° F. at night, and 10° higher in the daytime.

Among the favorite varieties for beginners are White Pride; Sleeping Beauty; Cavalier; Sparkling Red; and Startling.

Scindapsus aureus (Pothos; Joseph's oat; Devil's Ivy)

Some of the smaller varieties are decorative in the light-garden, although like so many foliage plants, they do not actually need a light-garden to live happily in the average living room. They are climbers, up or down, and are useful for covering the soil in pots that hold large plants; in softening the edges of stiff-looking planters; and to climb into the corners of the light-garden away from the direct light, to serve as background fillers. Keep them on the dry side, out of drafts and not too cold, with high humidity. Water them only with warm water, and cuttings should be watered sparingly until their roots are established. When you prune them, root the cuttings with bottom heat.

Senecio cruentus (Cineraria)

This is another of the popular gift plants that should be considered temporary. Enjoy it while it lasts, but don't try to save it or to propagate the seeds. One seed company says Cineraria is "impossible to propagate without a cool greenhouse," and the seeds are difficult at best, even if they germinate in their normal two to three weeks.

In the light-garden, treat Cineraria as a long-day plant that wants as much as sixteen hours of light, but set it under the ends of the tubes or on the edge of the shelf so that it does not receive too much light. It dislikes a hot, dry atmosphere, wants lots of water around its roots, and dries out fast. Temperature should not be above 60° F.

Sinningia speciosa (Gloxinia)

A gesneriad related to the African violet, Gloxinia culture is similar. It can be propagated from its very fine seed, sown without a covering layer on top of the vermiculite, misted into position, and will bloom in seven months. Or plant a tuber in February or March, for bloom during the summer and early fall. Keep it moist and warm, about 70° F., in rich, fibrous soil. The soil mixture recommended for African violets will be best. Place it about three inches below the ends of the fluorescent tubes in a pot just large enough to hold it until it becomes rootbound. Then transplant into a larger pot, begin to feed it regularly when in full growth, and increase its watering as it grows. Or you can propagate from leaf cuttings, either rooted in water or cut across the veins and pinned to the growing medium, as illustrated in chapter 6.

Normal blooming season for Gloxinias is summer and early fall, and they are most likely to bloom in the light-garden during that time, at least until you have altered their growth cycle. They need twelve to sixteen hours under lights, placed when mature about 8 inches below the tubes. If they tend to stretch toward the light, move them closer. After bloom, let them rest, and when dormant, you can divide the tubers.

Solanum Pseudo-Capsicum (Jerusalem Cherry; Christmas Cherry)

In the Johnston light-garden, the five-year-old Jerusalem Cherry is a highlight throughout the winter fruiting season (which follows its blooms); and again outdoors, when it blooms and fruits in the garden. The plant likes to be cool, in a humid atmosphere, with plenty of water around its roots. Shade-loving in the outdoor garden, it does best in the light-garden when placed off-center, where it does not receive too much direct light, about twelve inches below the tubes. It should not be allowed to become potbound.

It's always an intriguing project to sow seeds from plants like this that bears attractive fruits. Although it can be propagated easily from cuttings, taken early in the year, if you want to start seeds, dry them thoroughly first. Sow them in early February in a cool temperature, and pinch back occasionally before the first of July.

Succulents

Like cacti, succulents can easily be grown from seed, which is very fine and is best mixed with sand, sown on top of the sterile growing medium, and misted in. Water them sparingly because they don't like to be too wet. You can also propagate them easily from leaf cuttings, especially those varieties that have subsidiary buds on the edges of foliage. Rub both cutting and wound with powdered charcoal until it stops bleeding. They like an alkaline soil, live happily in people environment, and are undemanding. They prefer to be off-centered about 8 inches below the light in your light-garden, either on the shelf edges or under the ends of the tubes.

Tradescantia fluminensis (Wandering Jew; Inch Plant)

This quick-growing, moisture-loving plant will root anywhere, even in plain water, and is usually propagated from
cuttings. Take only those cuttings that are true to type, since
it tends to revert to green. The bright-leaved varieties should
be given a position fairly close to the light source in the light-
garden—a hanging basket a few inches below the ends of the
tubes is effective. If the foliage begins to become too green,
put the plant closer to the light.

We have found this an excellent plant for decorative purposes in the Johnston light-garden. And it's always nice to
have small vines that we can pot up in a hurry and give to
visitors.

Tropaeolum hybrids (Nasturtium) 6 to 8 inches; 12 to 20 inches.

If you want colorful flowers in a hurry, plant nasturtium
seeds. Sow them one-half inch deep in vermiculite, and with
bottom heat they should germinate in five days, to bloom in
about three months. The seeds are large enough to plant
easily and should be soaked before sowing. When the seedlings can be handled, pot them individually in poor soil in
peat pots without much fertilizer. Too much feeding will
produce greenery instead of flowers. If they are to stay permanently in the light-garden, transfer the seedlings directly
into their permanent pots, as they do not enjoy transplanting
too well. The dwarf types don't climb, and are ideal for
light-garden use. The climbing types are charming in hanging baskets in the light-garden, and we plant ours in the
outdoor garden against a wire trellis. By staggering the plantings, you can have a succession of light-garden bloom the
year round, but they will want to be kept fairly cool, despite
the fact that the first frost will kill their top growth. If you
want to carry them over from the outdoor garden for winter
bloom in the light-garden, take stem cuttings in early Sep-

tember, root them in vermiculite with a little fertilizer to give them a good start, and pot them up. They like full exposure to light when they are seedlings, but not so much when they are mature and blooming. So start the seedlings close to the lights with your sun-loving plants, directly under the center of the tubes, and move them out a bit to the edge when they come into flower. Outdoors, we grow them under trees, in almost constantly shaded rock gardens—or in full sun on a western slope.

Vinca rosea (Madagascar Periwinkle) annual, 10 to 20 inches

Seeds sown one-quarter inch deep about the first of March will produce plants that can bloom outdoors by July. For indoor light-gardening, seeds can be planted at any time, and expected to bloom in about four months. Or you can take leaf cuttings in March from established plants, so as to keep some in the light-garden while you set others outdoors. It makes a nice specimen plant, placed almost anywhere in the light-garden. It thrives well in either full sun (directly under the center of the lights) or in part shade (off at the ends or on the edge of the shelf).

Viola tricolor hortensis (Pansy; Heartsease) hardy annual, or bien., 6 to 8 inches

Although we buy pansy plants each spring as soon as they are available at the garden center, and set them out along the terrace even during a snow storm, they are said to be very easy to grow from seed. Our neighbor does it, and her plants are beautiful. Pansy seed tends to deteriorate rapidly, so you must start with seed that is guaranteed fresh. If you sow seeds collected from your own plants, sow them as soon as the pods have dried, about a week after you pick them. Scatter them over the top of your vermiculite, sprinkle over them just enough more vermiculite to cover them barely, and keep

them constantly moist and dark during their ten-day germination period. Don't put them under the lights until the seedlings have been up for ten days or so, then place them where
they will be out of the direct line of light intensity, well off-
centered and not closer than ten inches. As they grow taller,
transplant them into a half-sandy loam or a mixture of one
part peat moss to three parts garden soil, with good drainage.

Commercial plants for spring sales are usually started from
seed the previous August. But if you have fresh seed, you can
start them at any time and expect them to bloom within four
or five months if you treat the seedlings with care, as described. They should be kept, as mature plants, off-centered
in the light-garden, where they can have good air circulation and can be watered when necessary without getting too
much water on their foliage. During their early stages, before flowering, don't over-feed.

They tend to self-sow, to act as biennials, and sometimes
even to persist as perennials. It's our habit to treat them as
biennials, setting out fresh plants each year next to those we
planted last year. Some of last year's plants will bloom, and
we end up with a solid border of pansies that begins its bloom
in March or April and continues through the first several
frosts. It would not do so well, however, if we didn't keep
the blossoms picked; and in midsummer, when the plants
begin to stretch out into legginess, we prune them back drastically. It sets them back on their heels for a couple of weeks,
but after that they begin blooming again on somewhat shorter
stems and a little less profusely. They dislike a really hot
summer, and will retain their strength better if pruned in
this way.

In the Johnston borders, the pansies are dug out when the
dwarf marigolds are ready to bloom, and new plants are set
into the beds the following spring. But pansies are a Carrière
favorite, and we like to divide some up in early fall, to bring
into the light-garden for continued bloom. Next year, we'll
try seeds in the fall.

Zantedescha aethiopica (Calla Lily)

The dwarf varieties are practicable for the light-garden, and should be treated as any other bulb plant, described in chapter. It should be placed under the ends of the tubes or on the edge of the light-garden shelf, fed regularly and kept watered. It likes humidity in the atmosphere.

Zygocactus truncatus (Epiphyllum truncatum; Christmas Cactus; Crab Cactus)

Full-grown plants may become too large for the collection in a light-garden unless pruned back, but one can be set on a stand by itself as a specimen plant, with a 20-watt circular fluorescent setup suspended above it. Or it can be simply be placed near the light-garden, since it does not want high light intensity. Keep it moist and in a humid atmosphere, but between feedings, let it become a little drier around its roots. Give it less food and water after it has bloomed, and let it rest in a cool place until spring. (Naturally, it blooms for about two months around Christmastime.) Propagate by taking cuttings, rubbing both the cut end and the wound with powdered charcoal until they stop bleeding. Cuttings are best taken in September, potted in October when they have taken root. Like all of the cactus family, it is an easy plant to grow, adapting itself readily to whatever the environment may be.

Plants for the Gourmet

Kitchen gardens can be fun or a headache. Just don't plant too many seeds or buy too many young plants—just enough to ensure a supply of fresh herbs grown in your own indoor light-garden. You can also start your greens under lights, set them into the outdoor garden at the time your neighbors are planting seeds, and enjoy a harvest weeks earlier.

Popular herbs such as marjoram, chives, rosemary, thyme, oregano and others are included in the growing instructions for specific plants, listed according to their light-intensity preference. The following vegetables are some that we have grown successfully to setting-out size, and transplanted into the Johnston outdoor garden. There are many others that may appeal to you, and in general they can be grown for a longer period if given a light-garden start. As happens with flowering plants, purchased plants that cannot be set out immediately won't be lost if you hold them under the lights until it is convenient to put them into the ground.

Staggered planting of seeds is another excellent method for extending the growing and harvesting season. Vegetables that produce only one to a plant, such as carrots, radishes, beets and other root vegetables should be staggered two weeks apart, planting about one-quarter of the seeds in a single pack. In the same category are those vegetables like beans and peas, that produce for only two or three weeks in their entire harvest period. Staggered planting will produce crops straight through the summer.

Asparagus (peren.) 24 to 30 inches

Started from seed in the spring, placed about ten inches below the center of the lights when seedlings are an inch tall, you can begin to harvest asparagus within two years instead of waiting until the third year. The seedlings should be kept in the light-garden in sandy loam through the first winter, and set into the outdoor garden late in the second summer. You can expect to cut it the following spring.

Beans (annual)

Bush beans normally can be harvested in 50 to 57 days from seed planting. Pole beans take 60 days; and lima beans, 68 to 75 days. Each plant has a harvest period of two or three weeks, and to feed a family of four, you should plant seven to ten plants for each harvest period. According to the time you wish to begin harvesting, start fifteen to twenty seeds in vermiculite about a month ahead of outdoor planting time. When they have sprouted, set them in the light garden about six inches below the center of the tubes, and keep them there for a month. Two weeks after the first planting, if you start another fifteen or twenty seeds, you will have added an extra harvest period. Probably after the second set of plants has gone into the outdoor garden, you can begin planting successive batches two weeks apart directly into the outdoor soil.

Broccoli (annual)

Starting broccoli seeds indoors in early May and growing the seedlings under lights can give you edible cuttings from about the first of July instead of having to wait until fall. Harvest time begins about sixty days after the seeds are planted, and continues until frost. Broccoli needs rich, moist, sandy loam, and should not be set out until dependable warm weather has arrived.

Carrots (annual)

Staggered plantings are recommended for carrots if you are

fond of them, since there is only one to a plant. Seeds are planted two and a half months before you expect harvest. Start a first planting indoors about the first of April, set them out when the soil is warm in May, and you should begin to have a harvest by mid-June. Be sure to sow the seeds in sufficiently deep containers so that the carrots will have room to grow before you set them out. Keep them about eight inches under the end zones of the light-garden.

Cucumber, lemon (annual)

A two-week start in the light-garden produces cucumbers almost a month ahead of schedule. They should be ready to harvest in two months from the time you plant the seeds, and should not be set outdoors until the weather is warm. So if you start the seeds indoors about the first of May, give them two weeks in the light-garden under the center of the tubes about six inches below, set them out into sandy loam the first of June, you should have cucumbers all summer from late June or the first of July.

Eggplant (annual)

Start the seeds indoors about the first of May, and keep the seedlings eight to ten inches under the center of the lights for three weeks. They should be ready to eat by July.

Lettuce (annual)

Lettuce is one of the few plants that we have successfully germinated under lights without a dark period. Sow the very fine seeds on top of a bed of moist vermiculite, and do not cover the seeds. Press them gently into the growing medium, set them immediately into the light-garden, and set outdoors when seedlings are about two or three inches high. Plant two seeds for every head of lettuce you want, and stagger the sowings beginning 40 to 70 days before you expect your first cutting, according to the germinating and maturity time of the variety you have chosen.

Melon, Crenshaw (annual)

Melons can be set out by the first of June, and will be harvestable a month ahead of schedule if you start them in the light-garden in mid-April. Harvest is normally expected to begin 90 days after planting the seeds.

Onions (annual)

According to variety, onions are edible in 80 to 120 days after the seeds are planted. Start them indoors in the dark, transplant to sandy loam as soon as the soil is free of frost, and stagger the plantings. Two weeks in the light-garden gives them a very good start before they go outdoors.

Parsley (annual)

The curly variety is especially attractive for inclusion in the kitchen light-garden the year round. And it grows vigorously outdoors, of course. If you are an outdoor gardener in the summer with your light-garden out of operation, dig up a few plants before frost, and bring them back to continue growing under lights all winter. Start the seeds about the first of May, and set the seedlings six inches under the center of the lights if they are to go into the outdoor garden when the soil is frost-free. Start them any time if they are to remain permanently in the light-garden, and expect to be able to cut from them in two months.

Radish (annual)

Children enjoy growing radishes at any time of the year

under lights, because in three weeks from the seed-sowing time, radishes are edible. They are small enough to keep permanently in the light-garden, about six inches under the center of the tubes.

Spinach (annual)

Six weeks from seed planting, spinach can be cut and will continue to produce if you cut only the tender little leaves, leaving the older ones to feed the roots. Started the first of April, kept in the light-garden until frost has left the ground, and then set outdoors, it should be ready for cutting in June.

Tomatoes (annual)

According to varieties, tomatoes planted from seed will be ready to harvest in 55 to 80 days. By starting them in the light-garden eight inches below the center of the tubes, and setting them out when the soil is warm, you can have tomatoes a month ahead of schedule. Keep them picked, and you will have continued harvest all summer. For a family of four, you need no more than six plants.

FOR THE RECORD

If you have a permanent, year-round light-garden, only experience will tell you when to expect plants to bloom. As we have indicated in our general list, some that would bloom only once outdoors will bloom two or three times under lights. Others will follow their normal habits. Some will come into bloom faster than they would outdoors. Some will maintain their usual pace.

But blooming time under lights depends on when you start them, their degree of light sensitivity, the temperature in which they are grown, and their need for infra-red light. If they don't bloom when they have reached the age for blooming outdoors, as indicated on the general list, give them more warm white, or add the light from a couple of cool-burning, high-voltage incandescents.

Once you are satisfied that the lights you are using in your light-garden are what your plants need, a record of their blooming time and reactions will guide you in setting up a program that will keep your light-garden in colorful bloom all twelve months of the year. You will probably want at least this minimum of information on your record sheets:

PLANT (name or description)

FROM (where you got it)

PLANTED (when)
    (in what growing medium)
    (distance from lights)

CULTURE (watering and fertilizing, frequency and type)

RESULTS & COMMENTS (when it bloomed, etc.)

INDEX

183